# ◆◆ 本書の構成と特色 ◆◆

　本書は第一学習社発行の英文法準教科書「Zoom English Grammar 27 Lessons THIRD EDITION」に完全準拠したワークブックです。テキスト本体の練習問題を補充して，各項目の理解を助け，確実に学習事項が定着するように，次の構成で編集しています。

◆本課の **Drill** は，ドリル形式の基礎的な問題を中心に構成しました。学習の要点がつかめるよう，また，練習のヒントにもなるよう，各問題に「**ポイント**」を設けました。
◆**Exercises** は，空所補充・語形変化・書きかえ・英文和訳・整序作文など多彩な問題から構成され，総合的な英語力が身につくよう配慮されています。入試問題から成る **Try** を最終問として設けました。
◆効果的に学習が進められるよう，各問の指示文の末尾に，テキスト本体の解説項との対応関係( **A** **B** などで表示)を明示しています。

JN102716

# CONTENTS

# Get Ready 1 be-動詞の文と一般動詞の文

**1** （　　）内に，am，are，is から適語を選んで補いなさい。　**A**

1. I （　　　　　） 16 years old.　My sister （　　　　　） 20.
2. Jane and I （　　　　　） good friends.
3. This restaurant （　　　　　） very expensive.
4. You （　　　　　） my only friend.
5. These cases （　　　　　） very heavy.

**2** 次の文を指示に従って書きかえなさい。　**B**

1. I am very happy today. （否定文に）

2. This cake is delicious. （否定文に）

3. You are interested in football. （疑問文に）

4. John is angry with me. （疑問文に）

5. These are your books. （疑問文に）

**3** （　　）内に下の[　　]内から適切なものを選んで補いなさい。　**C**

1. My father （　　　　　） golf every weekend.
2. Some birds （　　　　　） to the south in the winter.
3. The tourist information center （　　　　　） at 9:00 in the morning.
4. She has many friends in foreign countries.　She （　　　　　） four languages.
   [fly, flies, open, opens, play, plays, speak, speaks]

**4** 次の文を指示に従って書きかえなさい。　**D**

1. I listen to the radio very often. （否定文に）

2. This plant grows in cold countries. （否定文に）

3. You want to be rich and famous. （疑問文に）

4. He lives near your house. （疑問文に）

5. Your father helps your mother in the kitchen. （疑問文に）

# Get Ready　2　過去の表現と未来の表現

**1** （　　）内に was または were を補いなさい。　Ａ

1. Steve （　　　　　） so happy yesterday.
2. We （　　　　　） in New York for two weeks last year.
3. He （　　　　　） not well yesterday, but he is better today.
4. （　　　　　） you angry with me? ── No, I （　　　　　） a little tired.

**2** 次の動詞の過去形を書きなさい。　Ｂ

1. clean　（　　　　）　　2. finish　（　　　　）
3. start　（　　　　）　　4. dance　（　　　　）
5. eat　（　　　　）　　6. leave　（　　　　）
7. find　（　　　　）　　8. stand　（　　　　）
9. do　（　　　　）　　10. tell　（　　　　）
11. have　（　　　　）　　12. know　（　　　　）
13. make　（　　　　）　　14. write　（　　　　）

**3** 次の文を指示に従って書きかえなさい。　Ｃ

1. We played tennis yesterday.　（否定文に）

2. I saw Mary at the party.　（否定文に）

3. Your brother passed the driving test.　（疑問文に）

4. You had a good time yesterday.　（疑問文に）

**4** 次の文を指示に従って書きかえなさい。　Ｄ

1. I am 16 years old.　（next weekをそえて，未来の文に）

2. We will be so busy next week.　（否定文に）

3. He will finish the report tomorrow.　（be going to ～を用いて）

4. We won't go out this evening.　（be going to ～を用いて）

5. It's going to rain soon.　（疑問文に）

# Get Ready　3　語順

**1** （　　）内の語句を並べかえ，英文を完成しなさい。　**A**

1. The lady (here / came / with Peter).

2. The train (at 9:30 / at Tokyo / arrived).

3. I (to the supermarket / went / yesterday).

4. Our cat (always / under the table / sleeps).

**2** （　　）内の語句を並べかえ，英文を完成しなさい。　**B**

1. (we / enjoyed / very much / the party).

2. (I / at the concert / some friends / met).

3. (passed / Ann / easily / the examination).

**3** （　　）内の語句を並べかえ，英文を完成しなさい。　**C**

1. My father (a young dog / gave / me) for my birthday.

2. He (gifts / sent / us) from England.

3. I'll (lend / my comic books / you) tomorrow.

4. Can you (me / pass / the salt), please?

**4** （　　）内の語句を並べかえ，英文を完成しなさい。　**D**

1. I (my driver's license / showed / the policeman / to).

2. They (a rich American / sold / the old vase / to) for $5,000.

3. I (gave / my ticket / the man / to) at the door.

4. Can you (lend / Mary / to / your bike)?

## Get Ready 4 修飾のパターン

**1** (　　) 内の語を補うべき箇所の直後の語を指摘しなさい。 **A**
1. Women wore dresses in the 18th century.　(long)
2. A wind blew from the north.　(cold)
3. Eat more fruit, vegetables, and salads.　(fresh)
4. George Washington was the president of the U.S.A.　(first)
5. Wood doesn't burn very well.　(wet)

**2** (　　) 内に下の [　　] 内から適切なものを選んで補いなさい。 **B**
1. Don't drive so (　　　　　).
2. Jane is studying (　　　　　) for her examination.
3. I'm tired this morning.　I didn't sleep (　　　　　) last night.
4. I carried the vase (　　　　　) in both hands.
5. The man laughed (　　　　　) at the joke.
   [carefully, fast, hard, loudly, well]

**3** 斜字体の語句が修飾している語 (句) に下線をつけ，和訳しなさい。 **C**
1. Please give me something *to eat*.

2. I went to a coffee shop *to meet a friend*.

3. The Internet is a way *to get information quickly*.

4. The baseball player jumped *to catch the ball*.

**4** 斜字体の語句が修飾している語 (句) に下線をつけ，和訳しなさい。 **D**
1. Do you know the boy *talking with Jim*?

2. All the people *eating in the restaurant* were tourists.

3. The cake *which Mary baked* was delicious.

4. This is one of the paintings *stolen from the museum*.

5. I got an email from a girl *who I've never seen*.

6. What's the name of the movie *which you saw yesterday*?

# Lesson 1 いろいろな文（1）

Drill

**1** 次の文を否定文と疑問文にしなさい。 **A**

1. You are good at swimming.

   否定文 : You（　　　　　）good at swimming.

   疑問文 : （　　　　　）（　　　　　）good at swimming?

2. This is Tom's notebook.

   否定文 : This（　　　　　）Tom's notebook.

   疑問文 : （　　　　　）（　　　　　）Tom's notebook?

3. The girls were absent from school.

   否定文 : The girls（　　　　　）absent from school.

   疑問文 : （　　　　）（　　　　）（　　　　　）absent from school?

☑be-動詞の文の否定文
主語＋be-動詞＋not … .
☑be-動詞の文の疑問文
Be-動詞＋主語 …?

**2** 次の文を否定文と疑問文にしなさい。 **B**

1. They went to Canada.

   否定文 : They（　　　　　）（　　　　　）to Canada.

   疑問文 : （　　　　　）they（　　　　　）to Canada?

2. That cat runs very fast.

   否定文 : That cat（　　　　　）（　　　　　）very fast.

   疑問文 : （　　　　）that cat（　　　　　）very fast?

3. Those girls play the piano.

   否定文 : Those girls（　　　　　）（　　　　　）the piano.

   疑問文 : （　　　　）those girls（　　　　　）the piano?

☑一般動詞の文の否定文
主語＋don't [doesn't, didn't]＋動詞の原形 … .
☑一般動詞の文の疑問文
Do [Does, Did]＋主語＋動詞の原形 …?

**3** 日本文の意味に合うように，（　　）内に適語を補いなさい。 **C**

1. 彼はいつその机を買ったのですか。

   （　　　　　）did he buy the desk?

2. それはどういう意味ですか。

   （　　　　　）does it mean?

3. あの背の高い男性はだれですか。

   （　　　　　）is that tall man?

4. あなたはなぜそんな質問を彼にしたのですか。

   （　　　　　）did you ask him such a question?

5. あなたは毎日どのようにして仕事へ行きますか。

   （　　　　　）do you go to work every day?

6. あなたのお気に入りの色は何ですか。

   （　　　　　）is your favorite color?

7. 彼らはいつ到着しましたか。

   （　　　　　）did they arrive?

☑who（だれ）／ what（何）／ which（どちら，どれ）／ when（いつ）／ where（どこ）／ why（なぜ）／ how（どのようにして）／ how many（どのくらい…か）

**1** 次の文を指示に従って書きかえなさい。　Ⓐ

1. He is an American student. （否定文に）

2. Your sister can play the piano. （疑問文に）

3. She was a nurse when she was young. （疑問文に）

**2** 次の文を疑問文にし，（　　）内の語を使って答えの文を書きなさい。　Ⓑ

1. You live in this house. （Yes）

2. Your father takes a walk every morning. （Yes）

3. Ann went to the library. （No）

**3** 下線部をたずねる疑問文に書きかえなさい。　Ⓒ

1. <u>Fred</u> broke the window.

2. She lost <u>the key</u>.

**4** （　　）内の語を並べかえ，英文を完成しなさい。　総合

1. なぜ彼女は昨日怒っていたのですか。
   (was / she / why / angry) yesterday?

2. だれがこの絵を描いたのですか。
   (painted / picture / this / who)?

**Try** 次の対話において，空欄に入れるのに最も適切なものを①〜④の中から選びなさい。

*A:* Where do you usually have lunch at your university?

*B:* （　　　　　）　　　　　　　　　　　　　　　　　〈武蔵野大〉

　① My mother usually makes lunch for me.

　② I usually buy dinner.

　③ We usually eat in one of the classrooms because the cafeteria is so crowded.

　④ My friends and I usually talk about our classes during lunch.

# Lesson 2 いろいろな文（2）

Drill

---

**1** 日本文の意味に合うように，（　　）内に適語を補いなさい。　A

1. トムはあなたのクラスメイトではないよね。—— はい，違います。
   Tom isn't your classmate, (　　　　　) (　　　　　)?
   —— (　　　　　), he (　　　　　).
2. トムとケンは早起きではありませんよね。—— いいえ，早起きです。
   Tom and Ken don't get up early, (　　　　　) (　　　　　)?
   —— (　　　　　), they (　　　　　).

✅**付加疑問文**
「…ですよね」
　肯定文，否定の疑問形？
「…ではありませんよね」
　否定文，肯定の疑問形？

---

**2** 日本文の意味に合うように，（　　）内に適語を補いなさい。　A

1. 兄弟はいないのですか。—— はい，いません。
   (　　　　　) you have any brothers? —— (　　　　　), I (　　　　　).
2. 外に出たくないのですか。—— いいえ，出たいです。
   (　　　　　) you want to go outside? —— (　　　　　), I (　　　　　).

✅**否定疑問文**
not を含む短縮形で始まる疑問文

---

**3** 日本文の意味に合うように，（　　）内に適語を補いなさい。　B

1. 彼女が昨日どこに行ったか知っていますか。
   Do you know (　　　　　) (　　　　　) (　　　　　) yesterday?
2. 彼がいつここに来るか教えてください。
   Tell me (　　　　　) (　　　　　) will (　　　　　) here.
3. だれが窓を割ったと思いますか。
   (　　　　　) do you think (　　　　　) the window?

✅**間接疑問文**
疑問詞の後は「S＋V」（平叙文の語順）になる。

---

**4** 例にならい，命令文を作りなさい。　C

(例) You don't study hard. ➡ Study hard.
　　 You use my pen. ➡ Don't use my pen.

1. You're not kind to old people.

2. You watch TV too much.

3. You are noisy here.

✅**命令文**
「〜しなさい」
　動詞の原形 …
「〜するな」
　Don't＋動詞の原形 …

---

**5** （　　）内に，How か What を入れて感嘆文を完成しなさい。　C

1. (　　　　　) beautiful that picture is!
2. (　　　　　) a beautiful picture that is!
3. (　　　　　) big eyes Yumi has!
4. (　　　　　) delicious coffee this is!
5. (　　　　　) hard your brother studied last year!

✅**感嘆文**
How＋形容詞[副詞]（＋S＋V）!
What (a [an]) (＋形容詞) ＋名詞 (＋S＋V)!

**1** （　　）内に適語を補い，日本文を英語に直して会話文を完成しなさい。　　A

1. Jane is an exchange student from the U.S.A., (　　　　) (　　　　)?
—— ええ，そうです。_____

2. Tom doesn't like reading novels, (　　　　) (　　　　)?
—— ええ，好きではありません。_____

3. (　　　　) you have a dictionary?　[あなたは辞書を持っていないのですか。]
—— いいえ，持っていますよ。_____

**2** 次の疑問文と（　　）内の語句をまとめて１文にしなさい。　　B

1. Where did I buy this dictionary?　(I don't remember ...)

2. How much is this camera?　(Can you tell me ...?)

3. What did he say?　(do you think ...?)

**3** 次の文を指示に従って書きかえなさい。　　C

1. You must be kind to others.　（命令文に）

2. You must not make a noise here.　（命令文に）

3. Your baby is very cute.　（感嘆文に）

**4** （　　）内の語を並べかえ，英文を完成しなさい。　　総合

1. 私はなぜ彼が怒っていたのかわからない。
I don't know (angry / was / he / why).

2. このことについては，昨日あなたにお話ししたでしょう。
(about / didn't / I / talk / to / you) this matter yesterday?

**Try** （　　）内の語を並べかえ，英文を完成しなさい。

1. メアリーが次に何をするつもりなのかはだれにもわからない。
(Mary / knows / what / do / will / nobody) next.　　〈関東学院大〉

2. 1日でどれくらい遠くまで行けると思いますか。
(you / can / go / we / think / far / do / how) in a day?　　〈青山学院大〉

9

# Lesson 3 文の型（1）

Drill

**1** 次の文の主語に＿＿を，（述語）動詞に＿＿を引きなさい。　A

1. Children in the world play with dolls.
2. The beautiful lady came here with her mother.
3. Every morning, my brother walks to his office.

> ☑ まず（述語）動詞が何であるかに注目する。

**2** 日本文の意味に合うように，（　　）内に［　　］内から適切な動詞を選んで補いなさい。　B

1. 彼は会議の間黙っていた。
   He (　　　　　) silent during the meeting.
   [grew, kept, seemed, sounded]
2. ついに，彼は科学者になった。
   Finally, he (　　　　　) a scientist.　[became, turned, made, got]
3. 彼女はとても忙しそうに見えた。
   She (　　　　　) very busy.　[saw, looked, made, became]
4. 彼女の話はそのとき本当には聞こえなかった。
   Her story didn't (　　　　　) true then.
   [hear, listen, think, sound]

> ☑ S＋V＋Cに用いられる主な動詞
> appear, look, seem ／ keep, stay, remain ／ become, get, go, grow, turn ／ feel, smell, taste, sound

**3** （　　）内の語句を並べかえ，英文を完成しなさい。　C

1. 私は彼女の電話番号を知りません。
   (don't know / her telephone number / I).

2. ジェーンは札幌でたくさんの写真を撮った。
   (a lot of pictures / Jane / took) in Sapporo.

3. トムと私はときどきこの部屋でピアノを弾きます。
   (Tom and I / the piano / sometimes play) in this room.

4. あなたはどこでその時計を買ったのですか。
   Where (buy / the watch / did / you)?

> ☑ S＋V＋O
> 「SはOをVする」
> 動詞の後に「…を」に当たる目的語がくる。

**4** 下線部の語句が目的語か補語かを答えなさい。　B C

1. It was cold yesterday.　(　　　　　)
2. The man smelled this apple.　(　　　　　)
3. This apple smells sweet.　(　　　　　)
4. She got the Nobel prize.　(　　　　　)
5. She doesn't look young.　(　　　　　)

> ☑ S＋V＋C
> S＝Cの関係
> ☑ S＋V＋O
> S≠Oの関係

**Exercises**

**1** 主語（S），動詞（V）を指摘し，全文を和訳しなさい。 **A**

1. That boy always studies hard.

2. The plane arrived at the airport half an hour ago.

3. The car in front of us stopped suddenly.

**2** 文中で下線部の語と＝の関係にある語を指摘し，全文を和訳しなさい。 **B**

1. The men in the room remained silent.　（　　　　　）

2. This cake tastes very nice.　（　　　　　）

3. The fresh snow looks beautiful on the hill.　（　　　　　）

**3** 主語（S），動詞（V），目的語（O）を指摘し，全文を和訳しなさい。 **C**

1. Margaret thanked me for my present.

2. What did you buy at the department store?

3. Power from the car engine turns the wheels.

**4** （　　　　）内の語句を並べかえ，英文を完成しなさい。 総合

1. 父は電車でオフィスに行く。

(my father / to / goes / train / his office / by).

2. 彼は腹が立ってきて，かんしゃくを起こしてしまった。

He (and / angry / became / his temper / lost).

**Try** （　　　　）内を補うのに最も適切なものを①～④の中から選びなさい。

1. Mary felt (　　　　) when she heard the results of the exam.　〈甲南女子大〉
　① being happy　　② happy　　　　③ happily　　　　④ to be happy

2. We were able to (　　　　) a lot of photographs at the party.　〈拓殖大〉
　① take　　　　　② make　　　　　③ have　　　　　④ get

11

# Lesson 4 文の型（2）

Drill

**1** 日本文の意味に合うように，[　]内の語を適切な場所に入れて，全文を書きなさい。　**A**

1. 私のおばは花を私に送ってくれた。
   My aunt sent some flowers. ［me］

2. 私たちにあなたのノートを見せてください。
   Please show your notebook. ［us］

3. ジムはメアリーによい席を見つけてあげた。
   Jim found a nice seat. ［Mary］

4. 私たちの先生はときどき私たちに面白い話をしてくれる。
   Our teacher sometimes tells an interesting story. ［us］

> ☑S+V+$O_1$+$O_2$
> 「S は $O_1$（人）に $O_2$
> （物）を V する」
> V の後に2つの目的語
> がくる。

**2** （　）内の語句を正しく並べて，S+V+O+C の文を作りなさい。　**B**

1. I call (Rose / my dog).

2. I found (very interesting / ecology).

3. My mother always (clean / her room / keeps).

4. (open / leave / the window).

> ☑S+V+O+C
> 「S は O を C に［であ
> ると］V する」
> O=C の関係が成り立
> つ。

**3** 下線部の語句が目的語か補語かを答えなさい。　**A B**

1. She found the book easy. （　　　　　）
2. She found him the book. （　　　　　）
3. Tom always keeps his bike clean. （　　　　　）
4. What do you call this bird in English? （　　　　　）
5. He made his sons new desks. （　　　　　）

> ☑S+V+$O_1$+$O_2$
> $O_1$≠$O_2$ の関係
> ☑S+V+O+C
> O=C の関係

**4** （　）内の語句を並べかえ，英文を完成しなさい。　**C**

1. かごの中には5羽の鳥がいます。 (are / in the cage / five birds)
   There _____.
2. テーブルの下にかぎがあります。 (is / under the table / a key)
   There _____.
3. 公園には多くの人々がいました。 (a lot of people / were / in the park)
   There _____.

> ☑There+be-動詞+
> S ….
> 「…に S がいる［ある］」
> be-動詞の後にくる主
> 語に合わせて動詞の形
> を変化させる。

**Exercises**

**1** 主語（S），動詞（V），間接目的語（O₁），直接目的語（O₂）を指摘し，第3文型に書きかえなさい。 **A**

1. My grandmother taught me the alphabet.

2. George's sister made him some sandwiches.

3. He bought his son a camera.

**2** 文中で下線部の語と＝の関係にある語を指摘し，全文を和訳しなさい。 **B**

1. Leave him <u>alone</u>. （　　　　　）

2. The parents named their baby <u>Daniel</u>. （　　　　　）

3. Alice found the movie <u>interesting</u>. （　　　　　）

**3** 次の英文を和訳しなさい。 **C**

1. There's a white building just around the corner.

2. Your meal is already on the table.

3. Jim's house is in the center of the city.

**4** （　　）内の語句を並べかえ，英文を完成しなさい。 **総合**

1. おばは私に美しいクリスマスカードを送ってくれた。
   My aunt (a / card / me / Christmas / beautiful / sent).

2. この近くに図書館はありませんか。
   (a library / there / here / is / near)?

**Try** （　　）内を補うのに最も適切なものを①〜④の中から選びなさい。

1. He found the variety show very (　　　　). 〈鹿児島大〉
   ① amused　　② amusing　　③ amusement　　④ amuse

2. At the end of this street, (　　　) a very big amusement park. 〈会津大〉
   ① theirs　　② it is　　③ it has　　④ there is

# Lesson 5 現在・過去・未来

Drill

**1** now を後ろにつけて，現在進行形の文にしなさい。 　A

1. Jim does his homework.

2. They don't listen to the radio.

3. Does Hideki play a video game?

✅現在進行形
「～している」
am [are, is] + ～ing
否定形は be-動詞に
not をつける。

**2** （　）内の語句を後ろにつけて，過去進行形の文にしなさい。 　B

1. It rained heavily.　（at that time）

2. Mary and Ichiro studied math.　（at that time）

3. Did she look at the picture?　（at that time）

4. Ms. Nakamura didn't cook.　（when he came）

✅過去進行形
「～していた」
was [were] + ～ing
否定形は be-動詞に
not をつける。

**3** （　）内の語句を後ろにつけて，will を使った未来の文にしなさい。 　C

1. It is cloudy.　（tomorrow）

2. We know the result.　（tomorrow）

3. Tom doesn't come to our concert.　（next weekend）

4. What do you cook for dinner?　（tomorrow）

✅will＋動詞の原形
未来のことがらや主語
の意志を表す。主語が
何であっても「will＋
動詞の原形」の形は変
わらない。

**4** 例にならい，be going to を使った文にしなさい。 　C

（例）I / buy a new car / next year
　　➡ I am going to buy a new car next year.

1. it / rain / tomorrow

2. Ken / come here / next week

3. I / buy some books / tomorrow

✅be going to＋動
　詞の原形
話者の主観的な判断
や意志・計画を表す。
be-動詞の形は主語に
合わせて変える。

**1** ( )内の動詞を現在形または現在進行形にし，全文を和訳しなさい。　**A**

1. I always (wear) boots when it rains or snows. (　　　　　)

2. Where is Jane? —— She (play) in the backyard. (　　　　　)

3. Please don't make so much noise. I (study). (　　　　　)

**2** ( )内の動詞を過去形または過去進行形にしなさい。　**B**

1. When I (enter) the room, he (talk) on the telephone.

2. When he (see) me, he (put) the receiver down.

3. When Tom (arrive), we (have) dinner.

**3** ( )内の動詞に will または be going to をつけ加えて適切な形にしなさい。　**C**

1. We don't have any salt. —— I (get) some from the shop then.

2. Your bicycle has a flat tire. —— I know. I (repair) it tomorrow.

3. There is somebody at the hall door. —— I (go) and open it.

**4** ( )内の語句を並べかえ，英文を完成しなさい。　総合

1. トムは毎朝シャワーをあびる。
   (a shower / every / Tom / morning / has).

2. 私たちはバスを待っていて，事故を目撃しました。
   We (the accident / we / saw / when / for / waiting / were) the bus.

**Try** ( )内を補うのに最も適切なものを①～④の中から選びなさい。

1. Something strange (　　　　) at school yesterday when we were having lunch.

〈立命館大〉

　① happened　　② happens　　③ is happened　　④ was happened

2. I (　　　　) play in a big soccer match next weekend.　〈熊本県立大〉

　① am going to　　② am going　　③ will to　　④ am will

## Lesson 6 現在完了形

Drill

**1** [　　　]内の語を使って現在完了形の文と，その否定文と疑問文を作りなさい。　A

1. You （　　　　　） （　　　　　） dinner.　[cook]
   否定文：You （　　　　　） （　　　　　） dinner.
   疑問文：（　　　　　） you （　　　　　） dinner?

2. Robert （　　　　　） （　　　　　） back to Singapore.　[go]
   否定文：Robert （　　　　　） （　　　　　） back to Singapore.
   疑問文：（　　　　　） Robert （　　　　　） back to Singapore?

3. The children （　　　　　） （　　　　　） all the oranges.　[eat]
   否定文：The children （　　　　　） （　　　　　） all the oranges.
   疑問文：（　　　　　） the children （　　　　　） all the oranges?

> **✔現在完了形**
> have [has] ＋ 過去分詞
> 否定形：haven't
> [hasn't] ＋過去分詞
> 疑問形：Have [Has]
> ＋主語＋過去分詞 …?

**2** [　　　　]内の語を使って現在完了形の文を作りなさい。　A

1. Yumi is charming, isn't she?　I like her. ── You are too late.
   I （　　　　　） （　　　　　） （　　　　　） a date with her.
   [already / get]

2. Will you return the money? ── What?　I （　　　　　） （　　　　　）
   （　　　　　） it to you.　[already / return]

3. Can I see your sister? ── She （　　　　　） （　　　　　） （　　　　　）
   out.　[just / go]

> **✔完了・結果「～し
> てしまった」**
> just（ついさっき），
> already（もう），yet
> （疑問文で「もう」，否
> 定文で「まだ」）などの
> 語句を伴うことが多
> い。

**3** （　　　）内に適語を補って現在完了形の会話文を完成しなさい。問いに対する答えは，（　　　）
内の日本語を参考にしなさい。　B

1. How many times （　　　　） （　　　　） （　　　　） that man?
   ── I have seen him （　　　　　）.　（1回）

2. How many times （　　　　） （　　　　） （　　　　） the video?
   ── I have watched it （　　　　） times.　（3回）

3. How many times （　　　　） （　　　　） （　　　　） that
   mountain?　── I have （　　　　） climbed it.　（一度もない）

> **✔経験「～したこと
> がある」**
> ever（かつて），never
> （一度も…ない），
> once（一度）などの語
> 句を伴うことが多い。

**4** （　　　）内に適語を補って現在完了形か現在完了進行形の文を作りなさい。〈　　　〉内の語は，
適切なほうを選びなさい。　C

1. Do you know Bill? ── Yes, I （　　　　　） （　　　　　） him 〈since,
   for〉 a long time.

2. Is Mary a teacher? ── Yes, she （　　　　　） （　　　　　） a teacher
   〈since, for〉 two years.

3. Is your mother working in the garden? ── Yes, she （　　　　　）
   （　　　　　） （　　　　　） in the garden 〈since, for〉 this morning.

> **✔継続「ずっと…だ
> [～している]」**
> since＋時の一点
> for＋時の長さ

**1** （　　）内の動詞を現在完了形にして，次の文の内容を表す文を作りなさい。　　　Ⓐ

1. Ann's hair was dirty.　Now it is clean.　(wash)

2. I can't remember her name now.　(forget)

3. Chris is looking for his room key.　He can't find it.　(lose)

**2** （　　）内の語句を使って，次の文の内容を表す現在完了形の文を作りなさい。　Ⓑ

1. Nora visited China in 1980 and 1985.　(twice)

2. I did not read *Hamlet*.　(never)

3. Susan really loves that movie and saw it a lot.　(see / eight times)

**3** 次の英文を和訳しなさい。　　　　　　　　　　　　　　　　　　　　　　　　Ⓒ

1. I have known Ms. Smith for eight years.

2. It's been raining since I got up this morning.

3. How long have you been staying in Kyoto?

**4** （　　）内の語を並べかえ，英文を完成しなさい。　　　　　　　　　　　　総合

1. 今までに日記をつけようとしたことがありますか。
   (ever / have / keep / to / tried / you) a diary?

2. どれくらい車いすを使っているのですか。
   (using / how / been / you / long / have) a wheelchair?

**Try** （　　）内の語句を並べかえ，英文を完成しなさい。

1. Recently, people (they / of / reduced / fish / have / the amount) eat in their diet.

〈札幌大〉

2. Mr. Smith, what (have / doing / been / to / looking / you / forward) in Japan?

〈東京経済大〉

# Lesson 7 過去完了形

Drill

**1** （　　）内に適語を補って，上の文を過去完了形の文に直しなさい。　A

1. The bus left.

The bus （　　　　　） （　　　　　　） when I got to the bus stop.

2. The baby fell asleep.

The baby （　　　　　） （　　　　　） asleep when her mother got home.

3. John had dinner.

John （　　　　　） （　　　　　） dinner when his parents got home.

4. Mike learned Japanese.

Mike （　　　　　） （　　　　　） Japanese when he went to live in Japan.

> ✅過去完了形
> had＋過去分詞
> 過去のある時点までの
> 「完了・結果」「経験」
> 「継続」を表す。

**2** 日本文の意味に合うように，（　　　　）内の動詞の一方を過去形に，もう一方を過去完了形に直して全文を書きなさい。　B

1. ケンはガールフレンドに，ネックレスを買ってあげたと言った。

Ken (tell) his girlfriend that he (buy) the necklace for her.

2. 彼らは仕事を終えてから帰宅した。

They (go) home after they (finish) their work.

3. 私たちは彼女が作ってくれていたクッキーを食べた。

We (eat) the cookies which she (make).

4. 警察が着いたとき，強盗は逃げてしまっていた。

The thief (run) away when the police (arrive).

5. 昨日，私はあなたが探していたかぎを見つけました。

Yesterday, I (find) the key you (are) looking for.

> ✅過去時制と過去完了形
> 過去完了形は過去時制よりも前の「時」を表す。

**3** 例にならい，下線部の動詞を過去形にして全文を書きなさい。　B

(例) Mr. Suzuki <u>thinks</u> that he is wrong.

　→ Mr. Suzuki thought that he was wrong.

1. Ken <u>says</u> that he will run faster than Tom.

2. I <u>know</u> that his story wasn't true.

3. Mary <u>tells</u> me that she has seen a tiger once.

> ✅時制の一致
> 主節の動詞が過去になると，ほかの動詞の時制も変化する。
> 現在時制→過去時制／
> will → would ／過去
> 時制→過去完了形／現在完了形→過去完了形

**Exercises**

**1** [ ]内の動詞を使って２番目の文を完成し，全文を和訳しなさい。　　　A

1. When we arrived at the party, John wasn't there.　He (　　　　　) home.　[go]

2. I recognized him at once.　I (　　　　　) him many times before.　[see]

3. He was out of breath.　He (　　　　　).　[run]

**2** (　　) 内の動詞を過去形または過去完了形にしなさい。　　　B

1. She was wearing a new hat.　She (buy) it the day before.

2. When I got home, I (find) someone (break) into my apartment.

3. I (catch) up with my friends who (leave) ten minutes before me.

**3** (　　) 内の語句を並べかえ，英文を完成しなさい。　　　総合

1. 私は金曜日のパーティーに行けると思った。
   (could / I / I / come / thought / party / the / to) on Friday.

2. その試合の前日まではとても暖かかった。
   (been / had / it / until / very / warm) the day before the game.

3. 彼女は３回グランドキャニオンに行ったことがあると私に言った。
   She told me (had / the Grand Canyon / to / she / been) three times.

4. チャーリーは私に会ったとジムに伝えると言った。
   Charlie said he (Jim / would / seen / had / tell / me / he).

**Try** (　　) 内を補うのに最も適切なものを①〜④の中から選びなさい。

1. The manager got angry because we (　　　　) finished the work by the deadline.
   〈学習院大〉

   ① had　　　② hadn't　　　③ have　　　④ haven't

2. I got the phone call when I (　　　　) dinner.　　　〈青山学院大〉
   ① have　　　② having　　　③ was having　　　④ had having

# Lesson 8 未来の表現

**1** ( )内を補うのに最も適切なものを選びなさい。　A

1. I ( ) my friends at 5 o'clock.
   (a) meet (b) am meeting (c) have met
2. Tom ( ) to Tokyo on business tomorrow.
   (a) is going (b) goes (c) went

> ☑未来を表す現在形
> 個人的に変更できない確定的な未来の予定を表す。
> ☑未来を表す現在進行形
> 近い未来の個人的な予定を表す。

**2** ( )内の動詞を現在時制か will ～ に直して全文を書きなさい。　B

1. Be careful! If you aren't careful, you (fall).

2. I'll telephone you as soon as I (get) there.

3. I (wait) until he arrives and then I (leave).

4. Stay here till the rain (stop).

5. Please hand this letter to her if she (come).

6. If the weather (be) fine tomorrow, we'll go on a picnic.

7. She (be) happy when she finds a good partner.

> ☑when [if] ＋現在時制
> 「時」や「条件」を表す副詞節では，未来のことも現在時制を用いて表す。

**3** ( )内の動詞を1.～4.は未来完了形に，5., 6.は未来完了進行形に直して全文を書きなさい。　C

1. If you don't hurry up, the restaurant (close) before you get there.

2. I (visit) Tokyo three times if I go there again.

3. I (be) in Paris for three years next month.

4. I (type) this report by the time you come back.

5. The baby (sleep) for an hour in ten more minutes.

6. I (teach) here for fifteen years next month.

> ☑未来完了形
> will have＋過去分詞
> ☑未来完了進行形
> will have been ～ing

**1** （　　）内を補うのに最も適切なものを選びなさい。　　　　　　　　　　A B

1. *A:* Have you seen John recently?

   *B:* No, but （　　　　　） lunch with him this weekend.

   (a) I am having　　　(b) I have had　　　(c) I have been having

2. I will take the train if it （　　　　　） tomorrow morning.

   (a) will rain　　　　(b) has rained　　　(c) rains

**2** （　　）内の語句を並べかえ，英文を完成しなさい。　　　　　　　　　B C

1. 明日のいまごろは，私たちはサンフランシスコに向けて出発しています。

   We (left / have / San Francisco / for / will) by this time tomorrow.

2. お客さんたちがここに着いてから，コーヒーを飲みましょうか。

   We'll have coffee (here / visitors / when / the / get).

**3** 斜字体の部分に注意して，和訳しなさい。　　　　　　　　　　　　　総合

1. There *is* a great tennis match tomorrow.　I *will be watching* it on TV at 9:00.

2. I *am meeting* my cousin at the museum at 1 o'clock.

3. Ted is working hard.　He *will have finished* the report by 8:00.

4. It *will have been snowing* a week if it *doesn't stop* tonight.

5. If I *have* time tomorrow, I'*ll do* some shopping downtown.

**Try** （　　）内を補うのに最も適切なものを①〜④の中から選びなさい。

1. *A:* Are you free tonight?

   *B:* I'm sorry, but （　　　　） dinner with my parents.　　　　　　〈奥羽大〉

   ① I had　　　　　　② I'm having　　　③ I've had　　　　④ I'd had

2. Richard will （　　　） biology and chemistry classes this year.　　〈南山大〉

   ① takes　　　　　　② taking　　　　　③ be taking　　　　④ to take

3. Please get in touch with me when you （　　　　） in Bangkok.　　〈獨協大〉

   ① arrive　　　　　　② will arrive　　　③ will be arriving　　④ arrived

# Lesson 9 助動詞(1)

Drill

---

**1** 次の文の下線部の動詞に can をつけて，全文を書きかえなさい。 **A**

1. I speak Spanish well.

2. The student runs one hundred meters in eleven seconds.

3. Linda dances the best of all the girls.

> ✔can 〜
> 「〜することができる」
> ＝be able to 〜
> can などの助動詞の後は，動詞は原形にする。

---

**2** 次の文の(　　)内に Can I か Can you のどちらかを補って文を完成しなさい。 **A**

1. （時間を知りたくて，時計を持っている人に対して）
   (　　　　　　　　) tell me the time, please?
2. （レストランでウェイターが客に向かって）
   (　　　　　　　　) take your order?
3. （食事中に，塩を取ってほしいときに）
   (　　　　　　　　) pass me the salt?
4. （靴屋で客が店員に）
   (　　　　　　　　) try these shoes on?

> ✔Can I 〜?
> 「〜してもよいですか」
> （許可を求める）
> ✔Can you 〜?
> 「〜してくれませんか」
> （依頼する）

---

**3** 日本文の意味に合うように，(　　)内に can, may のどちらかを補いなさい。 **A B**

1. 明日は雪かもしれません。　It (　　　　　) snow tomorrow.
2. あの川を泳いで渡れますか。　(　　　　　) you swim across the river?
3. 彼が俳優なんてことがあり得るだろうか。　(　　　　　) he be an actor?

> ✔can 〜
> 「〜することもありうる」
> ✔may 〜
> 「〜してもよい，〜かもしれない」

---

**4** 日本文の意味に合うように，[　　]内の語句から適切なものを選んで補いなさい。 **C**

1. ここでパスポートを見せなくてもいいですよ。
   You (　　　　　　　) show me your passport here.
   [must, must not, don't have to]
2. ケイトは弟の宿題を手伝わなければならない。
   Kate (　　　　　　　) help her little brother with his homework.
   [must, must not, doesn't have to]
3. 図書館では大声で話してはいけません。
   You (　　　　　　　) speak loudly in the library.
   [must, must not, don't have to]
4. ジムは顔色が悪い。気分が悪いにちがいない。
   Jim looks pale. He (　　　　　　　) be ill.
   [must, must not, doesn't have to]

> ✔must 〜
> 「〜しなければならない，〜にちがいない」
> ✔must not 〜
> 「〜してはならない」
> ✔don't have to 〜
> [don't need to 〜]
> 「〜する必要はない」

**1** ( ) 内に can (not) を補って文を完成し，全文を和訳しなさい。　[A]

1. Jack has traveled a lot.　He ( 　　　　 ) speak four languages.

2. ( 　　　　 ) I borrow your pen? —— Yes, of course.

3. That ( 　　　　 ) be Mary.　She's in the hospital.

**2** may を使って指示された英文を作りなさい。　[B]

1. Yes, you may take a photo of me.　（この文が答えとなる質問の文）

2. Where are you going for your holidays?　（「イタリアに行くかもしれない」と答える）

3. Ann is not feeling well.　（「今晩パーティーに来ないかもしれない」と言い足す）

**3** ( ) 内を英語に直し，文を完成しなさい。　[C]

1. You don't have enough time.　You (急がなくてはいけない).

2. Do we have plenty of time? —— Yes, we (急ぐ必要はない).

3. Is he British? —— Yes, he (英国人にちがいない).

**4** ( ) 内の語を並べかえ，英文を完成しなさい。　総合

1. もっとコーヒーを飲みませんか。
   (you / coffee / more / won't / have)?

2. 月曜日には会合があるかもしれない。
   There (be / meeting / a / on / may / Monday).

**Try** ( ) 内を補うのに最も適切なものを①〜④の中から選びなさい。

1. She ( 　　　 ) be over thirty; she must still be in her twenties.　〈京都学園大〉
   ① may　　　　② must　　　　③ oughtn't　　　④ can't

2. Miki and her family ( 　　　 ) out of town.　I have called several times, but there
   is no answer.　〈南山大〉
   ① could go　　② must be　　③ should go　　④ would be

# Lesson 10 助動詞（2）

Drill

**1** （　）内から正しいほうを選びなさい。　　　　　　　　　　　　　A

1. She (would / used to) often take a walk in the park.
2. There (would / used to) be two schools in this town forty years ago.
3. My grandfather doesn't smoke now, but he (would / used to) smoke every day.
4. He (would / used to) live in California.　He now lives in New York.
5. During the vacation, they (would / used to) often hike through woods.

> ☑would (often) ～
> 「かつては～したものだ」
> ☑used to ～
> 「（今は～しないが）かつては～した」
> 「かつては…だった」

**2** 例にならい，「～すべきでない」の意味の文を2つ作りなさい。　　　B

（例）eat too much　➡　You shouldn't eat too much.
　　　　　　　　　　　➡　You ought not to eat too much.

1. work too hard

2. watch too much TV

3. talk too loudly

> ☑should ～, ought to ～
> 「（当然）～するべきだ，～するはずだ」
> 否定形：
> shouldn't ～,
> ought not to ～

**3** 日本文の意味に合うように，[　]内の語を使って，（　）内に適語を補いなさい。　C

1. このひな鳥は巣から落ちたにちがいない。
　This baby bird (　　　　) (　　　　) (　　　　) from a nest.
　　　　　　　　　　　　　　　　　　　　　　　　　　[fall]
2. 彼はふだん乗っている電車に乗り遅れたのかもしれない。
　He (　　　　) (　　　　) (　　　　) his usual train.　[miss]
3. 彼女が英語の試験に失敗したはずはない。
　She (　　　　) (　　　　) (　　　　) the examination in English.　[fail]
4. 私たちはすばらしいときを過ごしました。あなたもそこにいるべきだったのに。
　We had a wonderful time.　You (　　　　) (　　　　) (　　　　) there.　[be]
5. 彼はもっと注意深くするべきだったのに。
　He (　　　　) (　　　　) (　　　　) (　　　　) more careful.　[be]

> ☑may have＋過去分詞
> 「～した［だった］かもしれない」
> ☑must have＋過去分詞
> 「～した［だった］にちがいない」
> ☑cannot have＋過去分詞
> 「～した［だった］はずがない」
> ☑should [ought to] have＋過去分詞
> 「～すべきだったのに（しなかったのは残念だ）」

**1** [   ]内の動詞に would または wouldn't を補って文を完成し，全文を和訳しなさい。 **A**

1. I loved swimming.  I (                    ) up early and go for a swim.  [get]

2. The key went into the lock, but it (                ).  [turn]

3. I have time.  I (               ) to play tennis in the afternoon.  [like]

**2** should または should not を使って，(    )内を英語に直して文を完成しなさい。 **B**

1. John has a cold.  He (学校に行くべきではない).

2. We have practiced tennis so hard.  We (試合に勝つはずだ).

**3** 次の文を指示に従って書きかえなさい。 **C**

1. He went shopping.  （may を使って「～したかもしれない」の文に）

2. Jane was asleep.  （must を使って「～していたにちがいない」の文に）

3. She did not see me.  （cannot を使って「～したはずがない」の文に）

4. Ken passed the examination.  （should を使って，「～したはずだ」の文に）

**4** (   )内の語を並べかえ，英文を完成しなさい。 総合

1. パーティーにおいでになりませんか。
   (to / you / would / come / like) to the party?

2. マークの送別会では楽しい時を過ごしました。君も来るべきだったのに。
   We had a good time at Mark's farewell party.  You (us / have / joined / should).

**Try** (   )内を補うのに最も適切なものを①～④の中から選びなさい。

1. I rarely eat ice cream now, but I (        ) it when I was a child.  〈城西大〉
   ① used to eat      ② was used to eating      ③ was used to eat      ④ used eating

2. I cannot find my smartphone.  I may (        ) it in the bus this morning.  〈南山大〉
   ① have been left     ② be left          ③ have left          ④ leave

# Lesson 11 受動態（1）

Drill

**1** 次の文を受動態にしなさい。　A

1. Mary cleans the room every day.

2. Shakespeare wrote *Hamlet*.

3. You find koalas in Australia. （by ... は不要）

✓受動態の作り方
①能動態の目的語
　→受動態の主語
②能動態の動詞
　→be-動詞＋過去分詞
③能動態の主語
　→by ...

**2** 次の英文を和訳しなさい。　B

1. What was invented by Thomas Edison?

2. Who was the electric light bulb invented by?

3. Why are young people employed at the company?

✓疑問詞＋受動態の疑問文

**3** それぞれの下線部を主語にした受動態の文に書きかえなさい。　C

1. Mr. Long teaches us history.
   We _____.
   History _____.
2. Tom sent Ann a nice present.
   Ann _____.
   A nice present _____.
3. The noise kept me awake all night.
   I _____.

✓S＋V＋O₁＋O₂の受動態
O₁を主語とするものと，O₂を主語とするものの二通りが可能。
✓S＋V＋O＋Cの受動態
Oを主語とし，Cは動詞の後にそのまま残す。

**4** 日本文の意味に合うように，[　　]内の表現を使って，（　　）内に適語を補いなさい。　C

1. その老婦人は，病院から来た看護師に世話をされた。
   The old woman （　　　　）（　　　　）（　　　　） by a nurse
   from the hospital. [care for]
2. その古新聞は今朝捨てられた。
   The old newspapers （　　　　）（　　　　）（　　　　） this
   morning. [throw away]
3. その子どもたちは，おばあさんに育てられた。
   The children （　　　　）（　　　　）（　　　　） by their
   grandmother. [bring up]

✓群動詞の受動態
群動詞をひとつの動詞として扱う。

Exercises

**1** 次の文を受動態にしなさい。 A

1. My father built this house in 1999.

2. They heard the music at the party from far away.

**2** 次の英文を和訳しなさい。 B

1. Who was bitten by a dog this morning?

2. Who was this building designed by?

**3** 日本文の意味に合うように，（　　）内に適語を補いなさい。 C

1. 会議は来週の日曜日に延期されるかもしれません。
   The meeting may be put (　　　　) till next Sunday.
2. これはよい考えだが，実行できない。
   This is a good idea, but it cannot be carried (　　　　).
3. その家は老婦人が面倒を見ている。
   The house is looked (　　　　) by an old woman.

**4** （　　）内の語を並べかえ，英文を完成しなさい。 総合

1. 彼女はその男性に話しかけられた。
   She (spoken / by / to / was) the man.

2. 彼女は友だちみんなから笑われた。
   (of / she / fun / made / was) by all her friends.

3. 彼は学校のサッカーチームのキャプテンに選ばれた。
   (elected / was / he / captain) of the school soccer team.

**Try** （　　）内を補うのに最も適切なものを①〜④の中から選びなさい。

1. The annual workshop of my company is usually (　　　) in December. 〈会津大〉
   ① holds　　　② holding　　　③ held　　　④ to hold
2. Unique insects (　　　) in rain forests and in deserts. 〈立命館大〉
   ① are finding　　② are found　　③ find　　　④ have found

# Lesson 12 受動態（2）

Drill

**1** 次の文を受動態にしなさい。 A

1. You must write the answers on the paper.

2. Someone has spilt some ink on the carpet.

3. Someone was playing the piano far too loudly.

> ✔ 助動詞を含む文の受動態
> 助動詞＋be＋過去分詞
> ✔ 完了形の受動態
> have [has, had] been＋過去分詞
> ✔ 進行形の受動態
> be-動詞＋being＋過去分詞

**2** 日本文の意味に合うように，下の(a)～(g)から適切なものを選んで記号を記入しなさい。 B

1. 彼はその光景に驚いた。
   He was surprised (　　　　　).
2. 彼は物理学に興味がある。
   He is interested (　　　　　).
3. 彼女は二等賞に満足していない。
   She is not satisfied (　　　　　).
4. その道は氷で覆われ，今日とても危険だった。
   The roads were covered (　　　　　) and were very dangerous today.
5. 私の母はすぐれた教師としてみんなに知られている。
   My mother is known (　　　　　) as a good teacher.
6. この家は木造です。
   This house is made (　　　　　).
7. 私たちはお母さんからのプレゼントを気に入りました。
   We were pleased (　　　　　).

> ✔ by以外の前置詞を用いる受動態
> ひとつひとつイディオムとして覚えよう。

(a) to everyone　　　　(b) in physics　　　　(c) with ice
(d) with the second prize　　(e) of wood
(f) at the sight　　　　(g) with our mother's presents

**3** 次の各文が同じ意味になるように，(　　)内に適語を補いなさい。 C

1. They say that Arthur has 22 children.
   a. (　　　　) (　　　　) (　　　　) (　　　　　) Arthur has 22 children.
   b. Arthur (　　　　) (　　　　) (　　　　) have 22 children.
2. People believed that the sun went around the earth.
   a. (　　　　) (　　　　) (　　　　) (　　　　) the sun went around the earth.
   b. The sun (　　　　) (　　　　) (　　　　) go around the earth.

> ✔ They say that ... の受動態
> It is said that ... /
> ... is said to ～
> この二通りのパターンがある。

**1** 次の文を受動態にしなさい。　　　　　　　　　　　　　　　　　　　Ａ

1. We will not make a decision until the next meeting.

2. He has spent all his money on his car.

3. They are building two new bridges across the river.

**2** 次の文の（　　）内に適切な前置詞を補いなさい。　　　　　　　　　Ｂ

1. Ken is very pleased（　　　　　）his new car.

2. We were surprised（　　　　　）her behavior.

3. I'm tired（　　　　　）playing the piano.　Let's go outside.

**3** ［　］内の動詞を「受動態＋前置詞」にして（　　）内を補い，全文を和訳しなさい。　Ｂ

1. Mike's father（was　　　　　　　　　）the Vietnam War.　[kill]

2. I（was　　　　　　　）a shower.　[catch]

**4** 次の文を指示に従って書きかえなさい。　　　　　　　　　　　　　　Ｃ

1. It is believed that John is in New York.　（John で始めて）

2. It is reported that two people were killed.　（Two people で始めて）

**5** （　　）内の語を並べかえ，英文を完成しなさい。　　　　　　　　　総合

1. これからやってくる休暇のことでわくわくしていますか。

（about / are / excited / you）the coming vacation?

2. ゴミをここに捨ててはいけない。

The garbage（thrown / should / be / away / not）here.

**Try**（　　）内を補うのに最も適切なものを①〜④の中から選びなさい。

1. When he heard the news, he（　　　　）that he couldn't say a single word.　〈広島工大〉
　① so surprised　　② was so surprised　　③ had so surprised　　④ was so surprising

2. She（　　　　）to have been one of the greatest scientists of the 20th century.　〈立命館大〉
　① believes　　② has believed　　③ is being believed　　④ is believed

# Lesson 13 不定詞（1）

Drill

**1** 下線部が主語・補語・目的語のうち，どの働きをしているかを答えなさい。　A

1. They decided to go by plane.　（　　　　　）
2. To see is to believe.　（　　　　　）
3. To obey the laws is everybody's duty.　（　　　　　）
4. I hope to have a good time at Tom's party.　（　　　　　）
5. My pleasure is to listen to pop music.　（　　　　　）

> ☑to-不定詞が「～すること」という意味を表す場合。

**2** 斜線の箇所のどちらかに（　）内の語句を入れて，文を完成しなさい。　A

1. It is / important / a promise.　(to keep)

2. He / hoped / a professional soccer player.　(to be)

3. His job / is / students English.　(to teach)

4. It is refreshing / a walk / early in the morning.　(to take)

5. I want / alone / all over Japan someday.　(to travel)

6. It was exciting / the famous actor / .　(to meet)

> ☑to-不定詞の名詞用法
> 主語として，補語として，目的語としての働きをする。

**3** （　）内の語句の動詞をto-不定詞にして前の文につなぎ，文を完成しなさい。　B

1. You should take something.　(read in the train during your trip)

2. She has a lot of friends.　(support her when she is in trouble)

3. He kept his promise.　(help me)

4. She has the ability.　(speak three languages)

> ☑to-不定詞の形容詞用法
> 「～する（ための）…」
> 「～する人[物]」
> 「～する（という）…」

**4** （　）内の語句を並べかえ，英文を完成しなさい。　B

1. メアリーは，結婚式に着て行くための新しいドレスを買った。
   Mary bought (to / wear / a new dress) to the wedding.

2. すぐに洗うべき服がたくさんある。
   There are a lot of (wash / to / clothes) right away.

> ☑to-不定詞の形容詞用法
> (代)名詞の後に続き，(代)名詞を修飾する。

**Exercises**

**1** 次の文の内容を to-不定詞を使い，（　　）内で始まる文に直しなさい。　　　　　　A

1. She has a dream to study in France.　（Her dream is …）

2. I will visit India.　（I plan …）

3. They will move out of the apartment.　（They have decided …）

**2** [　]内に示した内容を to-不定詞にして（　　）内を補い，全文を和訳しなさい。　　B

1. I want something (　　　　　　　　　). ［that I can eat］

2. The first country (　　　　　　　) the World Cup was Uruguay.　［that won］

**3** （　　）内の語句を並べかえ，英文を完成しなさい。　　　　　　　　　　　　　　総合

1. 新しい友だちをつくるのは難しいとわかった。
   I found (difficult / make / friends / it / new / to).

2. 私には今日すべき宿題がたくさんあります。
   I (a lot of / have / do / to / homework) today.

3. 彼女には何か冷たい飲み物が必要だ。
   She needs (to / drink / cold / something).

4. 毎日運動をすることは大切です。
   (it / get / exercise / important / to / is) every day.

5. 私の夢は，ヨーロッパ中を電車で旅することです。
   (dream / to / my / around / is / travel) Europe by train.

**Try** （　　）内を補うのに最も適切なものを①〜④の中から選びなさい。

1. Travelers found (　　　　) difficult to communicate without using a translation device.　　　　　　　　　　　　　　　　　　　　　　　　　　　　〈名城大〉
   ① itself　　　　② yourselves　　③ they　　　　　④ it

2. My mother found (　　　　) difficult to use her newly purchased smartphone.
   　　　　　　　　　　　　　　　　　　　　　　　　　　　　　　　　　　〈広島工大〉
   ① them　　　　② that　　　　　③ it　　　　　　④ one

参 p. 148−151

Drill

**1** 日本文の意味に合うように，（ ）内に適語を補いなさい。　Ａ

1. 100歳まで長生きする人もいます。
   Some people live （　　　　　）（　　　　　　　） one hundred years old.
2. 彼は音楽を勉強するためにイタリアに行くことに決めた。
   He decided to go to Italy in order （　　　　　）（　　　　　　） music.
3. 目が覚めてみると，パトリックは病院にいた。
   Patrick awoke （　　　　　）（　　　　　　） himself in the hospital.
4. 彼は電話に出るために立ち上がった。
   He got up （　　　　　）（　　　　　　） the phone.
5. 彼は混雑する時間帯を避けるために早く出た。
   He left early so （　　　　　）（　　　　　）（　　　　　　） the rush hour.

> ☑to-不定詞の副詞用法
> 「〜するために」（目的）
> 「…してその結果〜」（結果）

**2** 日本文の意味に合うように，（ ）内に適語を補いなさい。　Ｂ

1. そんなことをするなんて，あなたは不注意でしたね。
   You were careless （　　　　　）（　　　　　） that.
2. その知らせを聞いてうれしいです。
   I am glad （　　　　　）（　　　　　） the news.
3. 台所に黒い猫がいるのを見つけて驚いた。
   I was surprised （　　　　　）（　　　　　） a black cat in the kitchen.
4. きみはそんな給料のよい仕事を得て運がよかったよ。
   You were lucky （　　　　　）（　　　　　） such a well-paid job.
5. 喜んで車でお宅にお送りします。
   I'll be glad （　　　　　）（　　　　　） you home.

> ☑to-不定詞の副詞用法
> 「〜して」（感情の原因）
> 「〜するとは」（判断の根拠）
> 「〜するのが」（形容詞を限定）

**3** 例にならい，（ ）内の語が to-不定詞の意味上の主語になるように補いなさい。　Ｃ

（例）It is dangerous to swim in this river. （children）
　　➡ It is dangerous for children to swim in this river.

1. It is necessary to learn a foreign language. （us）

2. It was kind to come all the way to meet me. （you）

3. It is natural to say so. （him）

4. It was nice to give up your seat on the bus to the old woman. （you）

> ☑for / of を使って to-不定詞の意味上の主語を表す。
> It is ... for A to 〜
> 「Aが〜することは…だ」
> It is ... of A to 〜
> 「〜するとはAは…だ」

**1** 右の(a)〜(d)から適切なものを選び，文を完成しなさい。　　　　　　　　　A

1. He stood on a chair (　　　　　　).　　　　(a) in order to reach the top shelf
2. She ran down the street (　　　　　　).　　(b) so as not to miss the bus
3. He awoke (　　　　　).　　　　　　　　　　(c) to make a pie
4. We picked apples (　　　　　　).　　　　　(d) to find the house on fire

**2** (　　)内に示した内容をつけ加えて，to-不定詞の文を作りなさい。　　　　B

1. I was delighted.　(I got your letter last week.)

2. You took me to the station.　(You were nice.)

3. Some words are difficult.　(translate)

**3** 次の英文を和訳しなさい。　　　　　　　　　　　　　　　　　　　　　　C

1. It is dangerous for an old man to run fast.

2. It was nice of you to take me to the airport.

**4** (　　)内の語を並べかえ，英文を完成しなさい。　　　　　　　　　　　総合

1. 私はみんなに危険を警告するために叫んだ。
   I shouted (everyone / of / the / warn / danger / to).

2. ジェーンの筆跡はきちんとしていて読みやすい。
   Jane's writing (and / easy / is / neat / read / to).

3. 私をコンサートに招待してくださるとは，あなたはとてもご親切ですね。
   It (to / is / very / of / kind / invite / you) me to the concert.

**Try** (　　)内を補うのに最も適切なものを①〜④の中から選びなさい。

1. I didn't tell people I was coming, so they were totally surprised (　　　　) me.

   〈慶應義塾大〉

   ① by seeing　　② see　　　　③ seeing　　　④ to see

2. It was necessary (　　　　) me to stand up and speak out right away.　　〈宮崎大〉

   ① for　　　　② of　　　　③ to　　　　④ with

33

# Lesson **15** 不定詞（3）

Drill

---

**1** 例にならい，文を完成しなさい。

（例）Don't go.  （I told him ...）

　　→ I told him not to go.

1. Do your best.  （I want you ...）

2. Stay home.  （She asked me ...）

3. Don't use too much sugar.  （She advised him ...）

4. The children were quiet.  （I told the children ...）

A

☑S+V+O+to-不定詞
want+O+to-不定詞
「Oに～してもらいたい」
tell+O+to-不定詞
「Oに～しなさいと言う」
ask+O+to-不定詞
「Oに～してほしいと頼む」
to-不定詞の動作をするのはOである。

---

**2** （　　）内の語句を並べかえ，英文を完成しなさい。

1. Mr. Green （his son / made / wash） the car.

2. My father （go / let / me） camping with Jim.

3. Mary （carry / had / Tom） her heavy baggage upstairs.

4. I （cross / saw / the man） the road.

5. I didn't （come / hear / you） in.

6. I （felt / shake / the house）.

7. She （get off / the passengers / watched） the bus.

B

☑使役動詞＋O＋動詞の原形
「Oに～させる」
☑知覚動詞＋O＋動詞の原形
「Oが～するのを知覚する」

---

**3** 次の文を too ... to ～ か ... enough to ～ を用いて書きかえなさい。

1. I was so tired that I could not get up this morning.
   I was _____ .
2. The boy was so tall that he could touch the ceiling.
   The boy was _____ .
3. My mother is getting so old that she cannot travel.
   My mother is getting _____ .
4. He is so fat that he cannot dance.
   He is _____ .

C

☑too ... to ～ /
　... enough to ～
too ... to ～ は否定の意味を含む。「～するには…すぎる，…すぎて～できない」
... enough to ～ は肯定の意味を含む。「～できるほど（十分に）…，（十分に）…なので～できる」

**1** 次の文に「人＋to-不定詞」を使って（　　）内に示した内容を続けなさい。　　　　Ａ
1. We expected (Tom would be late.).

2. They warned (I didn't touch anything.).

3. We persuaded (Our neighbors turned the music down.).

4. I expect (He will win the race.).

5. I think (She is a genius.).

**2** 次の文の内容を下線部を補って完成しなさい。　　　　Ｂ
1. She wouldn't allow her children to go out in the rain.
   She wouldn't let ........................................................................................................ .
2. The official caused me to fill in a form.
   The official made ........................................................................................................ .
3. The man left the building.
   John saw ........................................................................................................ .

**3** （　　）内の語句を使って，次の質問に答える文を作りなさい。　　　　Ｃ
1. Shall we take a photograph?　(too dark)
   No, it is ........................................................................................................ .
2. Why don't we sit in the garden?　(warm enough)
   It's not ........................................................................................................ .

**Try** （　　）内を補うのに最も適切なものを①〜④の中から選びなさい。
1. This traffic is terrible. Why didn't I listen to my friend when she told me
   (　　　　) the train?　　　　　　　　　　　　　　　　　　　　　〈慶應義塾大〉
   ① take　　　　　② taking　　　　　③ to take　　　　④ took
2. Miho's parents won't let her (　　　　) to the concert.　　　　〈慶應義塾大〉
   ① go　　　　　② going　　　　　③ to go　　　　④ to going
3. The review made me (　　　　) to go and see that movie.　　　〈立命館大〉
   ① to want　　　② want　　　　③ wanted　　　④ wanting

**1** （　）内の語のどれかを選び，適切な場所に入れて，文を完成しなさい。　A

1. Could you tell me to get to the station?　(what, how, where)

2. Could you tell me to get on the bus?　(where, what, who)

3. I don't know to do next.　(why, what, who)

4. Will you tell me way to go?　(which, where, how)

5. Could you advise me to go or not?　(where, whether, why)

6. Have you decided to leave here?　(when, where, why)

> ☑疑問詞＋to-不定詞
> what to 〜／who to 〜／which to 〜／when to 〜／where to 〜／how to 〜／whether to 〜 (or not)

**2** 次の各組の文がほぼ同じ意味になるように，（　）内に適語を補いなさい。　B

1.
It seems that my uncle is more interested in literature than in history.
My uncle (　　　) (　　　) (　　　) more interested in literature than in history.

2.
It seems that she is a hard worker.
She (　　　) (　　　) (　　　) a hard worker.

3.
It seems that he knows everything.
He (　　　) (　　　) (　　　) everything.

4.
It seems that he finished his work.
He (　　　) (　　　) (　　　) (　　　) his work.

> ☑seem to 〜
> 「〜のようだ」の意味で，It seems that ... で書きかえられる。

**3** 次の英文を和訳しなさい。　C

1. I am anxious to see my lawyer at once.

2. You are certain to need help.

3. The child is eager to have the candy.

4. You are free to do what you like.

5. It is likely to be hot in August.

> ☑to-不定詞を含む慣用表現
> ひとつひとつイディオムとして覚えよう。

**1** （　　）内を英語に直し，文を完成しなさい。　　　　　　　　　　　　　Ａ

1. Tom explained to me （交換のしかた） the tire.


2. I asked him （どこに行くべきか）.


3. I don't know （何をあげたらいいか） Mary for her birthday.


**2** （　　）内の語句を主語にして，次の文を書きかえなさい。　　　　　　　Ｂ

1. It seems that the phone is out of order.　（The phone）


2. It seems that he has lost weight.　（He）


3. It appeared that the baby was hungry.　（The baby）


**3** 次の英文を和訳しなさい。　　　　　　　　　　　　　　　　　　　　　　Ｃ

1. I am unable to answer your question.


2. She was unwilling to tell us her name.


3. He was sure to win the race, and he did.


**4** （　　）内の語句を並べかえ，英文を完成しなさい。　　　　　　　　　　総合

1. 税務署の人が間違えたらしい。

　The tax people （made / seem / a mistake / have / to）.


2. だれに助けを求めたらいいかわからなかった。

　I was not sure （help / ask / to / who / for）.


**Try** （　　）内を補うのに最も適切なものを①〜④の中から選びなさい。

1. The man claims （　　　　） the ghost of a woman in the castle at night.　　〈福岡大〉

　① to have seen　　② to seeing　　③ to have been seen　　④ to be seen

2. The last question on the final exam was very difficult.　Can you explain （　　　　）

　to solve it?　　　　　　　　　　　　　　　　　　　　　　　　　　　〈秋田県立大〉

　① how　　　　　② why　　　　　③ what　　　　　　④ who

# Lesson 17 動名詞（1）

Drill

**1** 下線部が主語・補語・動詞の目的語・前置詞の目的語のうち，どの働きをしているかを答えなさい。

A

1. Swimming and jogging are both good for your health.　（　　　　）
2. Her hobby is gardening.　（　　　　）
3. Jim left the room without saying goodbye to anyone.　（　　　　）
4. Did you finish painting your house?　（　　　　）
5. Eating too much makes me sleepy.　（　　　　）
6. I don't mind waiting a few minutes.　（　　　　）
7. I am looking forward to seeing you soon.　（　　　　）

> ✔動名詞
> 名詞の働きをし，主語，補語，動詞の目的語，前置詞の目的語となる。

**2** （　　）内の動詞を動名詞か to-不定詞にしなさい。

B

1. She enjoys (play) tennis.　（　　　　）
2. We've decided (leave) here.　（　　　　）
3. He seemed shy, and he avoided (meet) our eyes.　（　　　　）
4. He wants (become) an artist.　（　　　　）
5. He promised (help) me.　（　　　　）
6. Would you mind (help) me carry this box?　（　　　　）
7. The boys refused (listen) to me.　（　　　　）
8. I can't imagine (be) late for school.　（　　　　）

> ✔to-不定詞しか目的語としない動詞
> want, hope, decide など
> ✔動名詞しか目的語としない動詞
> enjoy, finish, deny, mind など

**3** 日本文を参考にして，適切なほうを選びなさい。

C

1. 私はあなたの手紙を忘れずに投函するつもりです。
   I'll remember (to post / posting) your letter.
2. 私は以前どこかで彼女に会った覚えがある。
   I remember (to see / seeing) her somewhere before.
3. 寒いですよ。忘れずにコートを着るのですよ。
   It is cold.　Don't forget (to wear / wearing) your coat.
4. 彼がモーツァルトを演奏するのを聞いたことを私は決して忘れない。
   I will never forget (to hear / hearing) him play Mozart.
5. あなたの申し出は断られたということを残念ながらお知らせします。
   I regret (to inform / informing) you that your application has been refused.
6. 14歳で学校をやめたことを私は後悔しています。それは大きな間違いでした。
   I regret (to leave / leaving) school at fourteen.　It was a big mistake.
7. あなたの手紙を出すのを忘れていました。
   I forgot (to post / posting) your letters.

> ✔remember [forget, regret] ～ing
> 「（過去に）～したことを覚えている［忘れる，残念に思う］」
> ✔remember [forget, regret] to ～
> 「～しなければならないことを覚えている［忘れる，残念に思う］」

1　右の(a)〜(e)から適切なものを選び，文を完成しなさい。　A

1. Eating between meals (　　　　　).
2. My hobby is (　　　　).
3. Let's avoid (　　　　).
4. A vase is a kind of pot for (　　　　).
5. Check the oil before (　　　　).

(a) holding flowers
(b) is bad for the figure
(c) starting the car
(d) taking photos of night trains
(e) wasting time

2　(　　)内の動詞を動名詞か to-不定詞にしなさい。　B

1. I've tried many times to give up (smoke).　(　　　　)
2. She refused (work) for the enemy.　(　　　　)
3. It's cold.　Do you mind (close) the window?　(　　　　)
4. He has put off (make) a decision until tomorrow.　(　　　　)
5. She was only pretending (be) asleep.　(　　　　)
6. Have you finished (clean) the bathtub?　(　　　　)

3　日本文を参考にして，適切なほうを選びなさい。　C

1. 忘れずに宿題をするのですよ。
   Don't forget (to do / doing) your homework.
2. 私は目を開けていようとしたが，できなかった。
   I tried (to keep / keeping) my eyes open, but I couldn't.
3. 私はピアノのレッスンをやめてしまったことをいつも後悔しています。
   I've always regretted (to give / giving) up my piano lessons.

4　(　　)内の語句を並べかえ，英文を完成しなさい。　総合

1. 私の父はそれほど料理がうまくない。
   My father (cooking / at / isn't / good / very).

2. 台所の掃除が終わったら，買い物に行くつもりです。
   I'll go shopping (cleaning / have / I / when / the kitchen / finished).

Try　(　　)内を補うのに最も適切なものを①〜④の中から選びなさい。

1. My biggest mistake was (　　　) in the wrong direction because I got some old information.　〈西南学院大〉
   ① have gone　② gone　③ go　④ going
2. I suggested (　　　) pizza for lunch but my sister wanted something else.　〈東京電機大〉
   ① it make　② that makes　③ to make　④ making

# Lesson 18 動名詞（2）

Drill

**1** 例にならい，次の各組の文がほぼ同じ意味になるように，（　）内に適語を補いなさい。A

(例) { He is proud that his sister is a police officer.
He is proud of (his) (sister [sister's]) (being) a police officer. }

☑動名詞の意味上の主語
名詞('s)＋動名詞
所有格[目的格]＋動名詞

1. { I'm sure that her son will succeed in inventing useful things.
I'm sure of (　　　) (　　　) (　　　) in inventing useful things. }

2. { Her mother insisted that he should make a speech for Tomomi.
Her mother insisted on (　　　) (　　　) a speech for Tomomi. }

3. { Do you mind if I open the window?
Do you mind (　　　) (　　　) the window? }

**2** 例にならい，次の各組の文がほぼ同じ意味になるように，（　）内に適語を補いなさい。A

(例) { He was not aware that he had done anything wrong.
He was not aware of (having) (done) anything wrong. }

☑動名詞の完了形
having＋過去分詞の形で，動名詞の表す「時」が，述語動詞の表す「時」よりも「以前の時」であることを明示したいときに用いられる。

1. { She denied that she had told lies.
She denied (　　　) (　　　) lies. }

2. { She complained that she had been kept waiting.
She complained of (　　　) (　　　) kept waiting. }

3. { He was ashamed that he had made the same mistake.
He was ashamed of (　　　) (　　　) the same mistake. }

**3** 日本文の意味に合うように，下の(a)～(f)から適切なものを選んで記号を記入しなさい。B

☑動名詞を含む慣用表現
ひとつひとつイディオムとして覚えよう。

1. その計画は考えてみるだけの価値はあるよ。
The plan is (　　　).

2. 私を説得しようとしても無駄ですよ。
(　　　) to persuade me.

3. 今晩はビールを飲む気分ではありません。
I don't (　　　) beer tonight.

4. すべての人間が平等であることを否定することはできない。
(　　　) that all men are created equal.

5. お金で幸福を買えないことは言うまでもない。
(　　　) money cannot buy happiness.

6. その知らせが本当だとわかるとすぐに，彼女は突然泣きはじめた。
(　　　) the news true, she began to cry suddenly.

(a) worth considering　(b) There is no denying
(c) feel like drinking　(d) It is no good trying
(e) On finding　(f) It goes without saying that

**1** （　　）内に示した内容を動名詞にして，文を完成しなさい。　　A

1. I dislike (People ask me personal questions.).

2. Do you mind (I am sitting here.)?

3. My aunt is proud of (Her son won first prize.).

**2** 日本文の意味に合うように，（　　）内に適語を補いなさい。　　A

1. 彼はそこにいなかったと言った。
   He denied (　　　　　) (　　　　　　) there.
2. 人を訪ねるのは訪ねられるよりも楽しい。
   Visiting people is nicer than (　　　　　) (　　　　　　).
3. その少年は定刻に仕事に来なかったことで首になった。
   The boy was fired for (　　　　　) (　　　　　　) to work on time.

**3** 次の文と（　　）内の表現をまとめて 1 文にしなさい。　　B

1. Don't try to escape.　(It is no use ～ing.)

2. I can't deny that she is very efficient.　(There is no ～ing.)

3. Don't study if you're feeling tired.　(There is no point in ～ing.)

**4** （　　）内の語を並べかえ，英文を完成しなさい。　　総合

1. 彼はリンダが彼にうそをつこうとしたことに怒った。
   He was angry at (Linda / him / to / trying / lie / to).

2. もっと早くあなたのお手紙に返事をさしあげなかったことをお許しください。
   Please excuse me for (having / letter / not / your / answered) sooner.

**Try** （　　）内を補うのに最も適切なものを①〜④の中から選びなさい。

1. If you are planning to travel in France, stay in Lyon for a couple of days.　The city
   is known for its historical buildings, which are well worth (　　　　). 〈秋田県立大〉
   ① visit　　　　② visited　　　　③ visiting　　　　④ visitor
2. Jim's parents don't like the idea of (　　　　) part-time. 〈東海大〉
   ① he works　　② him to work　　③ his working　　④ to work

# Lesson 19 分詞（1）

Drill

**1** 例にならい，次の2つの文を分詞を用いて1文にしなさい。

☑名詞を修飾する分詞
現在分詞「〜している…」
過去分詞「〜された…」

（例）Do you know the girls?　They are playing in the park.
　　→ Do you know the girls playing in the park?

1. Who are those people?　They are waiting outside.

2. I talked to the man.　He was selling food.

3. I spoke to the woman.　She was standing on the corner.

4. The tests were very difficult.　They were given to the students.

5. The machine has not arrived.　It was ordered from England.

**2** 例にならい，文を完成しなさい。

☑知覚動詞＋O＋分詞
知覚動詞＋O＋現在分詞「Oが〜しているのを知覚する」
知覚動詞＋O＋過去分詞「Oが〜されるのを知覚する」

（例）He was lying in front of the sofa.
　　→ She found him lying in front of the sofa.

1. Jim was playing the violin.
　 I heard _____ .
2. Her husband was knocked down by a bus.
　 She saw _____ .
3. Your name was repeated.
　 I heard _____ .
4. He was shouting in the crowd yesterday.
　 I heard _____ .

**3** 例にならい，文を完成しなさい。

☑have [get] ＋O＋過去分詞
「Oを〜してもらう」（使役）
「Oを〜される」（被害）

（例）My hand was caught in the door.
　　→ I had my hand caught in the door.

1. His photograph was taken on his 90th birthday.
　 He had _____ .
2. His nose was broken in a fight.
　 Jack had _____ .
3. These dresses were cleaned.
　 Please have _____ .
4. A cake was made for her son's birthday.
　 Mary had _____ .

42

**1** 次の2つの文を分詞を用いて1文にしなさい。　　　　　　　　　　　　　A

1. The man was taken to the hospital.　He was injured in the accident.

2. Grandmother sat by the fire.　She was surrounded by her grandchildren.

3. They found the lifeboat.　It was floating upside down.

**2** 次の2つの文を分詞を用いて1文にしなさい。　　　　　　　　　　　　　B

1. I heard you.　You were arguing with your brother.

2. I saw a fox.　It was running through the woods.

**3** （　　）内の動詞を分詞に変え，全文を和訳しなさい。　　　　　　　　　C

1. I had my photos (take) by Tom.　（　　　　　　）

2. He had his hat (blow) off by a strong wind.　（　　　　　）

3. Didn't you get your hair (cut) today?　（　　　　　）

**4** （　　）内の語句を並べかえ，英文を完成しなさい。　　　　　　　　　総合

1. 火の手が上がるのが見え，人々が叫んでいるのが聞こえた。
   I (and / flames / heard / people / rising / shouting / saw).

2. あなたは月に何回散髪しますか。
   How many times (cut / do / have / you / your hair) a month?

**Try** （　　）内を補うのに最も適切なものを①〜④の中から選びなさい。

1. We had our house (　　　　) into last night.　　　　　　　　〈青山学院大〉
   ① broken　　　　　② to break　　　　③ break　　　　④ breaking

2. You can find information on our new products in the catalogues (　　　) every
   three months.　　　　　　　　　　　　　　　　　　　　　　　〈東海大〉
   ① distributed　　② distributing　　③ are distributing　④ are distributed

3. My son was almost asleep when he heard his name (　　　　).　　〈明治大〉
   ① call　　　　　② called　　　　③ calling　　　④ to be called

Lesson **20** 分詞（2）

Drill

**1** 下線部を分詞構文にして，全文を書きなさい。 A B

1. As he heard a noise, he looked toward the door.

2. When she found her lost ring, she jumped for joy.

3. Because he was tired from work, he went to bed early.

4. When the earth is seen from the moon, it must look like a ball.

5. We stood chatting for one hour and we forgot to go shopping.

6. Because they didn't know the way, they soon got lost.

7. As I didn't want to make any mistakes, I paid careful attention.

> ✓分詞構文
> 同じ主語・同じ時制で表される2つの文の一方を，分詞で始まる句で表現する。
> ✓分詞構文の作り方
> ①接続詞をとる。
> ②主語をとる。
> ③動詞を分詞にする。

**2** 例にならい，下線部を分詞構文にして，全文を書きなさい。 C

(例) Because it was very windy, Dave had to walk his bicycle.
　➡ It being very windy, Dave had to walk his bicycle.

1. Because it was sunny, Mary decided to sit out on the grass.

2. Because John was ill, Peter had to do two men's work.

3. Because there was nobody at home, Jim decided to go out.

4. After all the work was done, the men went home.

> ✓主語＋分詞構文
> 分詞構文の主語が主たる文の主語と異なる場合は，分詞の前に主語を置く。

**3** 日本文の意味に合うように，下の(a)〜(c)から適切なものを選んで記号を記入しなさい。 C

1. 概して男性のほうが女性よりも走るのが速い。
　(　　　　　　), men can run faster than women.

2. 最近の出来事から判断すると，政府の支持率は上がっているようだ。
　(　　　　　　) recent events, the government appears to be gaining in popularity.

3. 厳密に言えば，アメリカは西半球全体のことである。
　(　　　　　　), "America" means all of the western hemisphere.
　(a) Strictly speaking　　(b) Generally speaking　　(c) Judging from

> ✓慣用的な分詞構文
> ひとつひとつイディオムとして覚えよう。

**Exercises**

**1** （　　）内を分詞構文にして１文にしなさい。　　　　　　　　　　　　　　A B

1. (He was playing tennis.)　He hurt his arm.

2. The typhoon hit the city.　(It caused great damage.)

3. (She did not have a car.)　She found it difficult to get around.

4. (He was shocked at the news.)　He could not speak a word.

**2** 次の２つの文を分詞構文を用いて１文にしなさい。　　　　　　　　　　　C

1. We had spent almost all our money.　We couldn't stay at a hotel.

2. I have already seen the movie twice.　I don't want to go to the theater.

3. There was no vacant seat on the train.　I stood all the way.

**3** （　　）内の語を並べかえ，英文を完成しなさい。　　　　　　　　　　総合

1. あまり気分がよくなかったので，ジェイムズは横になることにした。
   (well / very / feeling / not), James decided to lie down.

2. ホテルを見つけてから，彼らは夕食の食べられる所をさがした。
   (hotel / found / having / a), they looked for somewhere to have dinner.

3. だれももう言うことがなかったので，会合は終わった。
   (any / say / nobody / to / having / more), the meeting was closed.

**Try**（　　）内を補うのに最も適切なものを①～④の中から選びなさい。

1. (　　　　) from the top of the hill, the giant rock looked like an old man's face.

〈広島工大〉

　① To see　　　② Seeing　　　③ Seen　　　④ Having seen

2. (　　　　) the story before, she didn't want to hear it again.　　〈京都産業大〉

　① Heard　　　② Being heard　　　③ Having heard　　　④ Having been heard

3. (　　　　) at the party, I noticed an old school friend I hadn't met for years. 〈立命館大〉

　① Arrived　　　② Arriving　　　③ Had I arrived　　　④ To be arriving

45

**1** 日本文の意味に合うように，空所に適語を補いなさい。　A

1. 私の母は見かけほど年をとっていない。
   My mother is (　　　　) (　　　　) old (　　　　) she looks.
2. 彼は私と同じくらい本を持っています。
   He has (　　　) (　　　) books (　　　) I have.
3. この馬はあの馬と同じくらい速く走ります。
   This horse runs (　　　) (　　　) (　　　) that horse.
4. 昨日ほど寒くありません。
   It isn't (　　　) (　　　) (　　　) yesterday.
5. フランクはジョンほどテニスが上手ではありません。
   Frank doesn't play tennis (　　　) (　　　) (　　　) John.
6. はちみつは，砂糖とほぼ同じくらい甘い。
   Honey is just about (　　　) (　　　) (　　　) sugar.

> ☑A ... as＋原級＋as B
> 「A は B と同じくらい ～である」
> ☑A ... not as [so] ＋原級＋as B
> 「A は B ほど～ではない」

**2** 下線部を主語にして，次の各文を〈A ... 比較級＋than B〉を用いて書きかえなさい。　A B

1. Tokyo isn't as old as Kyoto.

2. A notebook is not as light as this electronic dictionary.

3. Money is not as important as health and happiness.

> ☑A ... not as [so] ＋原級＋as B
> 「A は B ほど～ではない」＝B ... 比較級＋than A

**3** (　　)内の語句を並べかえ，英文を完成しなさい。　C

1. キリマンジャロはアフリカで一番高い山です。
   Kilimanjaro is (highest / the / in Africa / mountain).

2. ヒロが5人の中で一番背が高い。
   Hiro is (of / tallest / the / the five).

3. 大阪は日本で2番目に大きな都市です。
   Osaka is (second largest / the / city / in Japan).

4. サオリは私のサッカーチームで抜群によい選手だ。
   Saori is (player / best / by / the / far) on my soccer team.

5. メアリーはすべての科目の中で英語が一番好きだ。
   Mary likes (all subjects / of / the best / English).

> ☑the＋最上級＋in [of] ...
> 「…の中で一番～」

**Exercises**

**1** 日本文の意味に合うように，（　　）内に適語を補いなさい。 **A** **B**

1. ジョンは私と同じくらい早く起きる。

   John gets up (　　　　　) early (　　　　　) I.

2. アンは私ほど一生懸命に働かない。

   Ann does not work (　　　　　) (　　　　　) (　　　　　) I.

3. その映画はその本よりも面白かった。

   The movie was (　　　　　) interesting (　　　　　) the book.

**2** （　　）内の語句を並べかえ，英文を完成しなさい。 **C**

1. このホテルが町で一番安いです。

   This hotel is (town / cheapest / in / the).

2. フィレンツェが私の国では最も美しい都市です。

   Florence is (in my country / the / city / most beautiful).

3. サッカーはもっとも人気のあるスポーツの 1 つだ。

   Soccer is (most / of / one / popular / sports / the).

**3** （　　）内の語句を並べかえ，英文を完成しなさい。 総合

1. 私たちはあなたほど速くクロスワードパズルをすることができない。

   We can't do crosswords (quickly / as / you / as / do).

2. カリフォルニアはアメリカで 3 番目に大きな州だ。

   California (third / state / is / the / largest) in the United States.

3. その地震はその国が経験した最大の災害であった。

   The earthquake was (disaster / ever / experienced / greatest / had / that / the / the country).

**Try** （　　）内の語を並べかえ，英文を完成しなさい。

1. There are (Japan / more / in / people / than) in New Zealand. 〈大妻女大〉

2. According to United Nations world data, women live on (4.5 / than / average / years / longer) men. 〈昭和女大〉

参 p.218－225

Drill

**1** 例にならい，次の各文がほぼ同じ意味になるように，（　　）内に適語を補いなさい。 **A**

（例）Mt. Everest is the highest mountain.

    a. No other mountain is (as) high (as) Mt. Everest.

    b. No other mountain is (higher) than Mt. Everest.

    c. Mt. Everest is (higher) than (any) (other) mountain.

1. The Nile is the longest river in the world.

    a. No other river in the world is (　　　　) long (　　　　) the Nile.

    b. No other river in the world is (　　　　) than the Nile.

    c. The Nile is (　　　　) than (　　　　) (　　　　) river in the world.

2. Mary is the tallest girl in the class.

    a. No other girl in the class is (　　　　) tall (　　　　) Mary.

    b. No other girl in the class is (　　　　) than Mary.

    c. Mary is (　　　　) than (　　　　) (　　　　) girl in the class.

✅原級⇔比較級⇔最上級

最上級の意味合いは，原級，比較級を用いても表すことができる。パターンとして覚えよう。

**2** 日本文の意味に合うように，（　　）内に適語を補いなさい。 **B**

1. この箱の2倍の大きさのものがほしい。

    I want a box (　　　　) as large (　　　　) this.

2. 彼らの家は私たちの家のおよそ3倍の大きさである。

    Their house is about (　　　　) (　　　　) as big as ours.

3. 彼らの部屋は私たちの部屋の半分の大きさである。

    Their room is (　　　　) as large as ours.

4. この箱はあの箱の3分の2の大きさである。

    This box is (　　　　) as big as that.

5. あなたの車は私の車のおよそ1.5倍の大きさである。

    Your car is about (　　　　) and (　　　　) (　　　　) times as big as mine.

✅倍数表現

twice [... times, half, one-third, two-thirds] as＋原級＋as A

「Aの2倍［…倍，半分，3分の1，3分の2］」

**3** 例にならい，文を作りなさい。 **C**

（例）You finish your homework soon. / You can play soon.

    ➡ The sooner you finish your homework, the sooner you can play.

1. We leave soon. / We will arrive soon.

2. The weather is warm. / I feel good.

3. You have much. / You want much.

✅The＋比較級～，the＋比較級 ...

「～すればするほど，それだけいっそう［ますます］…」

Exercises

**1** 次の各組の文がほぼ同じ意味になるように，（　　）内に適語を補いなさい。 **A**

1. { August is the hottest month in Japan.
    （　　　　　） other （　　　　　） is （　　　　　） than August in Japan.

2. { Mary arrived earliest of all the girls.
    Mary arrived （　　　　　） （　　　　　） any other （　　　　　）.

3. { Tokyo is the largest city in Japan.
    No other city in Japan is （　　　　） （　　　　） （　　　　） Tokyo.

**2** 日本文の意味に合うように，（　　）内に適語を補いなさい。 **B**

1. ビルは中国についてできるだけ多くのことを学ぼうと決心した。
   Bill decided to learn （　　　　） much （　　　　） （　　　　） about China.

2. 彼女は作家というより哲学者だ。
   She is not （　　　　） （　　　　） a writer （　　　　） a philosopher.

3. 30人もの生徒が試験に落ちた。
   As （　　　　） as thirty students failed the exam.

**3** 次の英文を和訳しなさい。 **C**

1. The shorter the days become, the colder the weather gets.

2. More and more people are downloading music from the Internet.

3. This tie is the cheaper of the two.

**4** （　　）内の語を並べかえ，英文を完成しなさい。 総合

1. 私が予想していたよりも3倍の時間がかかった。
   It took (times / as / three / long / as) I had expected.

2. 最近とても忙しい。昔ほど暇な時間がない。
   I am very busy these days.　(have / spare / I / than / less / time) I used to.

**Try** （　　）内を補うのに最も適切なものを①〜④の中から選びなさい。

1. （　　　　） you spend, the more your English improves.　〈摂南大〉
   ① More time　　　② The more time　　③ Most time　　　④ The most time

2. As a college student, I want to read （　　　　）.　〈会津大〉
   ① as possible as many books　　　② as many as books possible
   ③ as many as possible books　　　④ as many books as possible

49

# Lesson 23 関係詞（1）

**1** 例にならい，次の2つの文を関係代名詞を使って1つの文にしなさい。 **A**

(例) This is the man.　He wanted to see you.

　　→ This is the man who wanted to see you.

☑who
先行詞が「人」の場合
☑which
先行詞が「物」の場合

1. This is the book.　It was on the chair.

2. Do you know anybody?　He / She wants to buy a car.

3. I met a man.　He knows you.

**2** 例にならい，次の2つの文を1つの文にしなさい。 **B**

(例) The dress is very pretty.　You are wearing it.

　　→ The dress you are wearing is very pretty.

☑目的格の関係代名詞は省略されることが多い。

1. The books are my brother's.　I lent them to you.

2. Did you get the pictures?　I sent them to you.

3. This is the story.　He wrote it.

**3** 例にならい，次の2つの文を関係代名詞を使って1つの文にしなさい。 **C**

(例) I met a girl.　Her parents worked in a hospital.

　　→ I met a girl whose parents worked in a hospital.

☑関係代名詞 who の所有格：whose

1. That's the man.　His house has burned down.

2. We met the man.　His son won the race.

**4** 例にならい，次の2つの文を関係代名詞 that を用いて1文にしなさい。 **D**

(例) This is the highest building.　We have it in the city.

　　→ This is the highest building that we have in the city.

☑thatが好んで用いられる場合
先行詞が「唯一」：the only ..., the same ..., the very ..., the first ..., the＋最上級 ...
先行詞が「全・無」：all ..., every ..., no ...

1. Don't believe anything.　He says it.

2. The captain was the last person.　He left the sinking ship.

3. This is the same watch.　I bought it in Tokyo.

**Exercises**

**1** 次の文の（　　）内から適切な関係代名詞を選びなさい。　　A B C
1. Correct the sentences (who / which) are wrong.
2. This is the longest novel (whom / that) I have ever read.
3. What's the name of the man (whose / who) car you borrowed?
4. The number of tourists (whom / who) visit Bali is increasing.
5. The bird (which / whom) was injured by a cat will get well soon.
6. Did you get the things (which / whom) you wanted?
7. This is a word (which / whose) meaning I don't know.

**2** 次の2つの文を関係代名詞を用いて1文にしなさい。　　A B
1. What was the name of the man?　He lent you the money.

2. Jim works for a company.　It makes computers.

3. The shoes are not very comfortable.　I'm wearing them.

**3** （　　）内の語を並べかえ，英文を完成しなさい。　　C
1. 表紙が赤のあの辞書は，ボブのものです。
   (cover / dictionary / is / red / whose / that) is Bob's.

2. この学校には母語が日本語ではない子どもたちだけが通っています。
   This school is only for children (first / is / Japanese / language / not / whose).

**4** 次の英文を和訳しなさい。　　D
1. I will give you everything you want.

2. This is the best chance that I have ever had.

**Try**　（　　）内を補うのに最も適切なものを①〜④の中から選びなさい。
1. I have a friend (　　　　) lives in New York.　　〈駒澤大〉
   ① who　　　② when　　　③ how　　　④ which
2. Several guests (　　　　) rooms had been broken into complained to the hotelkeeper.
   〈東邦大〉

   ① when　　　② what　　　③ that　　　④ whose

# Lesson 24 関係詞（2）

**1** 例にならい，what を用いて日本語の部分を英語に直して，文を完成しなさい。 **A**

（例）（あなたがしたこと）is the right thing.

➡ What you've done is the right thing.

> ☑関係代名詞 what
> 「〜すること［もの］」
> (=the thing(s) which)
> の意味で，それ自体に
> 先行詞を含んでいる。

1. He got （彼がほしいもの）.

2. Is this （あなたが探しているもの）?

3. Were you surprised at （彼が言ったこと）?

4. （彼が言うこと）is not important.

5. （彼が一番好きなこと）is just sitting in the sun.

6. Please show me （あなたが買ったもの）.

7. I cannot do （彼が私にしてほしいこと）.

**2** 次の文を和訳しなさい。 **A**

1. What he did is wrong.

> ☑ what A used to
> be「かつてのA」
> what is＋比較級
> 「さらに…なことには」

2. The guitarist is not what he used to be.

3. Beth plays the piano, and what is more, she can write songs.

**3** 例にならい，次の2つの文を1文にしなさい。 **B**

（例）The chair is broken.　You are sitting on it.

➡ The chair you are sitting on is broken.

> ☑（関係代名詞）…前
> 置詞
> 前置詞まで含めて先行
> 詞にかかっていくこと
> に注意。

1. Who is the woman?　You were talking to her this morning.

2. Isn't this the book?　You are looking for it.

3. That is the house.　I lived in it in my early days.

4. What's the name of the hotel?　You told me about the hotel.

**1** （　　）内に what または that を補いなさい。　Ⓐ

1. I won't tell anyone （　　　　） has happened.
2. She gives her children everything （　　　　） they want.
3. Why don't you explain （　　　　） you have in mind?
4. This is （　　　　） he says.
5. I won't be able to do much but I'll do the best （　　　　） I can.

**2** 日本文の意味に合うように，（　　）内に適語を補いなさい。　Ⓐ

1. 私が一番驚いたのは，彼が急に現れたことだった。
   （　　　　）（　　　　　） me most was his sudden appearance.
2. 彼女は裕福な男性と結婚した。彼女はいわゆる「シンデレラ」だ。
   She married a rich man.　She is （　　　　）（　　　　　）（　　　　） a "Cinderella."
3. さらに悪いことに，彼は酒におぼれた。
   （　　　　）（　　　　　）（　　　　　）, he has taken to drinking.
4. わたしが今日あるのは，両親のおかげです。
   My parents have made me what （　　　　）（　　　　） today.

**3** 日本文の意味に合うように，（　　）内に適切な前置詞を補いなさい。　Ⓑ

1. この子が私がコンサートへ一緒に行った男の子です。
   This is the boy I went to the concert （　　　　）.
2. ここは私のいとこがはたらいている病院だ。
   This is the hospital my cousin works （　　　　）.
3. 私たちが行ったパーティーはあまり面白くなかった。
   The party we went （　　　　） wasn't very enjoyable.
4. 彼が話している寺は清水寺のことです。
   The temple he is talking （　　　　） is the Kiyomizu Temple.

**Try** （　　）内の語句を並べかえ，英文を完成しなさい。

1. He (admired / for / is / what / doing) he says he will.　〈成蹊大〉

2. He is (a / called / human computer / is / what).　〈常葉学園浜松大〉

3. Tom's life has changed a lot and he is (ago / he / not / ten years / was / what).　〈獨協大〉

# Lesson 25 関係詞（3）

Drill

**1** 日本文の意味に合うように，（　　）内に適切な関係副詞を補いなさい。　**A**

1. 月曜日が私の暇な日です。
   Monday is the day （　　　　　） I am free.
2. あそこが交通事故のあった場所ですか。
   Is that the place （　　　　　） the traffic accident happened?

> ☑where
> 先行詞が「場所」の場合
> ☑when
> 先行詞が「時」の場合

**2** 例にならい，文を作りなさい。　**A**

（例）He didn't come for this reason. ➡ This is why he didn't come.

1. He was late for this reason.


2. The war broke out for that reason.


3. They were very polite for that reason.

> ☑why
> This is why ...「こういうわけで…」
> That is why ...「そういうわけで…」

**3** 日本文の意味に合うように，（　　）内に適語を補いなさい。　**B**

1. 妻のお母さんは，90歳ですが，英語を流暢に話す。
   My wife's mother, （　　　　　） is 90, speaks English fluently.
2. マーティンは，お父さんが日本人ですが，日本の漫画が大好きです。
   Martin, （　　　　） father is Japanese, loves Japanese comic books.
3. 京都は，私が生まれたところですが，古寺がたくさんあります。
   Kyoto, （　　　　　） I was born, has lots of old temples.
4. 日曜日は休みで，だれも仕事に行きません。
   Sunday is a holiday, （　　　　　） people do not go to work.
5. 彼は私の写真を破った。それにはびっくりした。
   He tore up my photo, （　　　　　） upset me.

> ☑関係詞の非制限用法
> 「先行詞，関係詞…」の形で，先行詞を追加説明する。
> ☑非制限用法のwhich
> 前の文の全体または句や節を先行詞とする用法もある。

**4** 日本文の意味に合うように，（　　）内に下の[　　]内から適切なものを選んで補いなさい。　**C**

1. だれが来ても歓迎されるでしょう。
   （　　　　　） comes will be welcomed.
2. 何度やってみても，答えがわからなかった。
   （　　　　　） often I tried, I could not find the answer.
3. 都合のよいときにいつでも来なさい。
   Come （　　　　　） it is convenient for you.
4. きみに関係があることは何でもぼくにも関係がある。
   （　　　　　） concerns you concerns me.
   [whenever, whoever, however, whatever]

> ☑複合関係詞
> 関係詞に-ever がついたもので，名詞節や副詞節を導く。ひとつひとつ意味を覚えておこう。

**Exercises**

**1** （　　　）内に適切な関係副詞を補い，全文を和訳しなさい。　　　　　　　　**A**

1. Do you know a restaurant (　　　　　　) we can have a really good meal?

2. 1945 was the year (　　　　　　) the Second World War ended.

3. The reason (　　　　　) I can't go is that I don't have time.


**2** 次の英文を和訳しなさい。　　　　　　　　　　　　　　　　　　　　　　　**B**

1. Smoking, which is a bad habit, is nevertheless popular.

2. I went to see the doctor, who told me to rest for a few days.

3. Jim passed his driving test, which surprised everybody.


**3** （　　　）内に適切な複合関係詞を補って，全文を和訳しなさい。　　　　　**C**

1. He told the story to (　　　　　) would listen.

2. People always want more (　　　　　　) rich they are.


**4** （　　　）内の語を並べかえ，英文を完成しなさい。　　　　　　　　　　総合

1. サマンサは電話番号を教えてくれて，私はそれを紙に書きとめた。
   Samantha told me her phone number, (wrote / on / which / down / I) a piece of paper.

2. 私の持っているものは何でもあなたのものです。
   (have / I / is / whatever / yours).


**Try** （　　　）内を補うのに最も適切なものを①〜④の中から選びなさい。

1. Do you remember the scene in the movie (　　　　　) the police officer finds the robber?
   ① for　　　　　② there　　　　　③ where　　　　　④ which　　　　〈関西学院大〉

2. Liverpool, (　　　　　) is in the north west of England, is famous as the hometown of
   the Beatles.　　　　　　　　　　　　　　　　　　　　　　　　　　　　　〈東海大〉
   ① why　　　　　② where　　　　　③ who　　　　　④ which

3. Children should eat (　　　　　) they are served by their parents.　　　〈駒澤大〉
   ① nonetheless　② which　　　　③ the way　　　　④ whatever

# Lesson 26 仮定法（1）

Drill

**1** [　]内の語を適切な形に直して，仮定法の文を作りなさい。 A

1. I don't have enough time.　If I (　　　　　) enough time, I
   (　　　　　) see you off at the airport.　[have / can]

2. That book is expensive.　If that book (　　　　　) not expensive,
   I (　　　　　) buy it.　[be / will]

3. You are not telling the truth.　If you (　　　　　) telling the truth,
   you (　　　　　) look me straight in the eye.　[be / can]

4. He speaks too fast.　If he (　　　　　) more slowly, people
   (　　　　　) understand him.　[speak / can]

5. I am not a good cook.　If I (　　　　　) a good cook, I (　　　　　)
   make all of my own meals.　[be / will]

6. There is no telephone here.　If there (　　　　　) one, we
   (　　　　　) call them up.　[be / can]

> ✅ 仮定法過去
> 現在の事実に反することを仮定
> If＋S＋過去形 …, S＋助動詞の過去形＋動詞の原形 …

**2** [　]内の語を適切な形に直して，仮定法の文を作りなさい。 B

1. I was sick.　If I (　　　　) not (　　　　　) sick, I would
   (　　　　) (　　　　　) out.　[be / go]

2. I didn't have a camera.　If I (　　　　) (　　　　　) a camera, I
   would (　　　　) (　　　　　) some pictures.　[have / take]

3. She had a headache.　If she (　　　　) not (　　　　　) a headache,
   she would (　　　　) (　　　　　) with us.　[have / come]

4. You didn't ask me for tickets.　If you (　　　　) (　　　　　) me
   for tickets, I could (　　　　) (　　　　　) some.　[ask / get]

5. I didn't know you were in the hospital.　If I (　　　　) (　　　　　)
   you were in the hospital, I would (　　　　) (　　　　　) you there.
   [know / visit]

> ✅ 仮定法過去完了
> 過去の事実に反することを仮定
> If＋S＋had＋過去分詞 …, S＋助動詞の過去形＋have＋過去分詞 …

**3** (　)内の語を並べかえ，英文を完成しなさい。 C

1. 万が一また失敗したら，あなたはどうしますか。
   (if / again / fail / should / you), what will you do?

2. 万が一明日雨が降れば，私たちは出発を延ばします。
   (if / tomorrow / rain / should / it), we'll put off our departure.

3. 万が一彼が電話をしてきたら，私は家にいないと言ってください。
   (if / call / he / should), tell him I am not at home.

> ✅ If＋S＋should 〜
> 未来のことを表す仮定法
> 「もしも（万が一）Sが〜すれば」

**Exercises**

**1** （　　）内の動詞を適切な形にしなさい。 　　　　　　　　　　　　　　　A

1. If she (know) your address, she would come and see you.

2. If you (have) a helicopter, you would be in time for the train.

3. If I (be) a bird, I would fly to you.

**2** 次の文を仮定法を使って書きかえなさい。 　　　　　　　　　　　　　　B

1. We didn't have a map, so we couldn't find out the waterfall.

2. I slipped on the ice, so I broke my arm.

3. We stayed at the hotel because George recommended it to us.

**3** 次の英文を和訳しなさい。 　　　　　　　　　　　　　　　　　　　　C

1. What would happen if you did not go to work tomorrow?

2. If I should be offered the job, I think I would take it.

3. If the sun were to stop rising, what would happen?

**4** （　　）内の語を並べかえ，英文を完成しなさい。 　　　　　　　　　総合

1. もしだれかがお金をたくさんくれたら，あなたはどうしますか。
   What would you do (somebody / a lot of / you / if / gave / money)?

2. もし万一あなたが病気になったら，私たちが病院の費用を払います。
   (you / fall / should / if / ill), we will pay your hospital expenses.

**Try** （　　）内を補うのに最も適切なものを①〜④の中から選びなさい。

1. The painting has turned out to be a fake.  If it were real, it (　　　　) millions of
   dollars. 　　　　　　　　　　　　　　　　　　　　　　　　　　　　〈玉川大〉
   ① cost 　　　　　　② costs 　　　　　　③ will cost 　　④ would cost

2. If I had not lost my file, I (　　　　) the job on time. 　　　　　〈立命館大〉
   ① had finished 　② have finished 　③ finished 　　④ would have finished

# Lesson 27 仮定法（2）

Drill

**1** 例にならい，次の各組の文がほぼ同じ意味になるように，（　　）内に適語を補いなさい。 A

（例）
- If I were in your place, I would call an ambulance.
- (Were) (I) in your place, I would call an ambulance.

> ✅ ifの省略と倒置
> if-節の if を省略して，主語と動詞を倒置する。（書き言葉）

1. 
- If I had been there, I would have spoken to him.
- (　　　　　) (　　　　　) been there, I would have spoken to him.

2. 
- If he had gone to Washington, he would have visited Mary.
- (　　　　　) (　　　　　) gone to Washington, he would have visited Mary.

3. 
- If I were in your position, I would take his offer.
- (　　　　　) (　　　　　) in your position, I would take his offer.

**2** 例にならい，次の各文を〈I wish＋仮定法〉の文に書きかえなさい。 B

（例）I can't speak Spanish. ➡ I wish I could speak Spanish.

> ✅ I wish＋仮定法
> 「…であればなあ」（現在[過去]の事実の反対を願望する。）

1. I don't like dancing.

2. You were not here yesterday.

3. I don't know his address.

4. I can't help you.

**3** 日本文の意味に合うように，下の(a)〜(e)から適切なものを選んで記号を記入しなさい。 B

> ✅ 仮定法を含む慣用表現
> ひとつひとつイディオムとして覚えよう。

1. もし新鮮な空気がなければ，私たちは健康を維持できないだろう。
   (　　　　　), we could not stay healthy.
2. もしあなたの助言がなかったら，私は総支配人として失敗していたかもしれない。
   (　　　　　), I might have failed as a general manager.
3. この薬がなかったら，私は死んでいたかもしれない。
   (　　　　　), I might have been dead.
4. 12時近くです。もう私たちは帰宅する時間です。
   It's nearly midnight. (　　　　　) we went home.
5. 私は子どもではないのに，ときどきあなたはまるで私が子どもであるかのように話をする。
   I'm not a child, but sometimes you talk to me (　　　　　).

   (a) it's high time
   (b) as if I were a child
   (c) if it had not been for your advice
   (d) without this medicine
   (e) if it were not for fresh air

Exercises

**1** 次の文を if を使って書きかえなさい。 A

1. Should it rain, the reception will be held indoors.

2. Had you taken a taxi, you would have got here on time.

3. An honest boy wouldn't tell a lie.

4. Ben studied hard; otherwise, he would have failed the test.

**2** 次の内容を表す文を指示に従って書きなさい。 B

1. It rains a lot in England, but I hate it. （I wish ... で始まる文に）

2. I need your advice, and I think you will give me some. （I hope ... で始めて）

3. It is a pity that I didn't bring my camera. （If only ... で始まる文に）

4. She is not my aunt, but she sometimes acts like my aunt. （as if ... を使って）

5. Without his wife's money, he'd never be a movie director. （If it ... で始まる文に）

6. I think we should do something about pollution. （It's time ... で始めて）

**3** （ ）内の語を並べかえ，英文を完成しなさい。 総合

1. 私たちがあのとき結婚していたらなあ。
   (had / we / married / only / if / got) at that time!

2. もしもその絵が本物なら，何千ポンドの値打ちがある。
   (genuine / the / were / picture), it would be worth thousands of pounds.

**Try** （ ）内を補うのに最も適切なものを①～④の中から選びなさい。

1. I wish I ( ) a phone call soon after he sent the email to me. 〈中央大〉
   ① could make　　② had made　　③ have made　　④ made

2. Had I known that Peter was having financial problems, I ( ) him. 〈南山大〉
   ① would help　　② would have helped　　③ will help　　④ have helped

# Optional Lesson 1 接続詞

**1** 次の文を（　　）内の語句を使って書きかえなさい。　　A

1. If you take my advice, you will win the match. （and）

2. He didn't write. He didn't telephone. （neither A nor B）

3. George bought a cell phone. His friends bought cell phones. （not only A but B）

**2** （　　）内に適切な接続詞を補い，全文を和訳しなさい。　　B

1. It surprised me （　　　　　） he was still sick in bed.

2. She made it clear （　　　　　） she was not interested.

3. We were surprised at the fact （　　　　　） he is blind.

4. It's hard to say （　　　　　） it's going to rain or not.

5. The fact is （　　　　　） his parents don't know anything about his plans.

**3** 日本文の意味に合うように，（　　）内から適切なものを選びなさい。　　C

1. 私たちはちょうど今はそんなに忙しくないのだから，休憩したらいいよ。
   (Since / Until) we're not very busy just now, you can take a rest.
2. もしあまり疲れていなければ，あなたと魚釣りに行きます。
   (When / Unless) I am too tired, I'll go fishing with you.
3. ロンドンにいるときは，ふつう私は演劇を見に行きます。
   (Because / When) I'm in London, I usually go to the theater.
4. あなたが行かせてくれるまで私は叫ぶのをやめませんよ。
   I won't stop shouting (until / when) you let me go.
5. おじいさんは80歳を超えているのに，まだとても元気にしている。
   (Although / Because) Grandpa is over eighty, he is still very active.

**Try** （　　）内を補うのに最も適切なものを①〜④の中から選びなさい。

1. Make sure you wash the dishes and turn off the lights （　　　　　） you go to bed. 〈南山大〉
   ① until　　　② before　　　③ during　　　④ while
2. （　　　　　） I hear from you within three days, I will have to postpone our meeting.

〈関西学院大〉

   ① While　　　② Although　　　③ Unless　　　④ Because

# Optional Lesson 2 話法

**1** 先月あなたは Bob に会いました。以下の彼の言葉を間接話法で書きなさい。 **A**

1. "My father is in the hospital."
   Bob said _____.
2. "I saw Jack at a party a few months ago."
   Bob said _____.
3. "I'm going to Canada next week."
   Bob said _____.

**2** 次の文を間接話法に書きかえなさい。 **B**

1. Emi said to me, "Can you come to dinner on Friday?"


2. I said to her, "Is Mr. Smith in?"


3. The woman said to Peter, "Why did you apply for the job?"



**3** 直接話法の文は間接話法に，間接話法の文は直接話法に書きかえなさい。 **C**

1. Ann said to me, "Please don't tell anyone about the accident."


2. She told me not to eat too much.



**4** （　）内の語句を並べかえ，英文を完成しなさい。 総合

1. ジムはロンドンでは彼のところに泊まりに来るように言ってくれた。
   Jim said that (could / stay / him / and / I / with / come) in London.


2. ジーンは私にショッピングセンターに行くかたずねた。
   Jean asked me (go / I / to / would / if / the shopping mall).


**Try** 次の各組の文がほぼ同じ意味になるように，（　）内に適語を補いなさい。

1. {
   "I never want to see you again!" she said to me.
   She (　　　　) me she never (　　　　) to see me again. 〈学習院大〉
   }
2. {
   I said to him, "Do you really want to see her?"
   I asked him if (　　　　) really (　　　　) to see her. 〈福島大〉
   }

# Optional Lesson **3** 名詞と冠詞

**1** ( )内を補うのに最も適切なものを選びなさい。　A

1. Do you want ( )?
   (a) a cup of a coffee　(b) a cup of coffee　(c) cup of a coffee　(d) cup of coffee
2. How ( ) can we take on the plane?
   (a) many baggage　(b) many baggages　(c) much baggage　(d) much baggages
3. They only got married recently and they haven't got ( ).
   (a) many furniture　(b) many furnitures　(c) much furniture　(d) much furnitures

**2** ( )内から正しいほうを選びなさい。　A

1. I had a part-time (job / work) while I was at college.
2. The sheep on the hillside made a peaceful (scene / scenery).
3. Can you give me any (information / informations)?
4. The desire for (money / moneys) is a cause of much unhappiness.

**3** ( )内を補うのに最も適切なものを選びなさい。　B C

1. Bill drinks five cups of coffee ( ).
   (a) a day　　　　　　(b) for a day　　　　　(c) in a day
2. The female lion is ( ) as the male lion.
   (a) as a good hunter　(b) as good a hunter　(c) a as good hunter
3. She lives in a special home for ( ).
   (a) an elderly　　　　(b) elderly　　　　　(c) the elderly
4. My friends live in a very beautiful house.　But ( ) has only a small kitchen.
   (a) a house　　　　　(b) its house　　　　(c) the house

**4** ( )内の語句を並べかえ，英文を完成しなさい。　総合

1. I'd like to (a punch / give / in / that fellow / the face).

2. He's (a / nervous / person / talk / to / too) in front of a large group of people.

**Try** ( )内を補うのに最も適切なものを①～④の中から選びなさい。

1. Please contact the school office for ( ).　　　　　　　　　　　〈清泉女大〉
   ① another information　　　② more informations
   ③ far more informations　　④ further information
2. That cook was ( ) that we didn't want to complain about the poor service.
   〈青山学院大〉

   ① so kindness a man　　　② so kindness of a man
   ③ such nice a man　　　　④ such a nice man

## Optional Lesson 4 代名詞

**1** ( )内に下の[ ]内から適切なものを選んで補いなさい。 **A**

1. Mary swam from one side of the river to ( ).
2. Some people like dogs and ( ) like cats.
3. If you don't like one doctor, you can ask to see ( ).
4. Two of them remained and all ( ) went out.
5. Have you ever seen a wolf? —— No, I've never seen ( ).
   [another, one, others, the other, the others]

**2** ( )内から正しいほうを選びなさい。 **B**

1. He was examined by three doctors, but (all / none) of them could find anything physically wrong.
2. (Each / Every) of the boys has his own job.
3. (All / Every) of the boys here can play soccer well.

**3** 各文の( )内に both, either, neither から適語を選んで補いなさい。 **C**

1. I bought two newspapers. Which one do you want?
   —— ( ). It doesn't matter which one.
2. I offered him coffee or tea, but he didn't want ( ).
3. Is today the 18th or the 19th?
   —— ( ). It's the 20th.
4. Did you go to Scotland or Ireland for your holidays?
   —— We went to ( ). A week in Scotland and a week in Ireland.

**4** ( )内の語句を並べかえ，英文を完成しなさい。 総合

1. Do you want (another / exchange / for / this toaster / to) or do you want your money back?

2. I have a few books on Chinese food. You (borrow / can / if / like / one / you).

**Try** ( )内を補うのに最も適切なものを①～④の中から選びなさい。

1. Some of our nursing students work for hospitals, ( ) for clinics around the country, and a few at elementary schools. 〈東海大〉
   ① the other ② other ③ others ④ the others
2. I don't like this jacket. Would you please show me ( )? 〈東京農業大〉
   ① another ② one ③ other ④ something

# Optional Lesson 5 形容詞と副詞

**1** ( )内を補うのに最も適切なものを選びなさい。　**A**

1. Harry doesn't like reading; he has ( ) books.
   (a) a few　　　(b) a little　　　(c) very few　　　(d) very little
2. A very sick child has ( ) strength and can eat only a little food.
   (a) a few　　　(b) a little　　　(c) few　　　(d) little
3. Is there any soup left? —— Yes, ( ).
   (a) a few　　　(b) a little　　　(c) very few　　　(d) very little

**2** ( )内に下の[ ]内から適切なものを選んで補いなさい。　**B**

1. I'm ( ) of sugar, so I'll go and buy some more.
2. He can drive quite well, but he's not ( ) at parking.
3. I'll give you a key, then you're ( ) to come and go as you please.
4. Unfortunately the government was very ( ) to react to the problem.
   [good, free, short, slow]

**3** ( )内を補うのに最も適切なものを選びなさい。　**C**

1. It is raining; ( ), I think the game will be played.
   (a) however　　　(b) moreover　　　(c) therefore
2. It's raining. ( ), the picnic is canceled.
   (a) Nevertheless　　　(b) Otherwise　　　(c) Therefore
3. Mary didn't want to go out for a walk. The weather was wet and miserable. ( ), she had a headache.
   (a) Besides　　　(b) Thus　　　(c) Yet
4. You'd better listen to me. ( ), things might go wrong.
   (a) However　　　(b) Moreover　　　(c) Otherwise

**4** ( )内の語句を並べかえ，英文を完成しなさい。　総合

1. Today, people (are / aware / is / that / the environment) in danger.

2. Ann is a fantastic tennis player. Jill is not very good. Ann is (at / better / much / tennis / than) Jill.

**Try** ( )内を補うのに最も適切なものを①〜④の中から選びなさい。

1. He used to spend so ( ) time playing video games.　　　〈日本大〉
   ① a lot　　　② a few　　　③ much　　　④ many
2. Your paper has to be at least ten pages long; ( ) you will be in trouble.
   ① and　　　② nevertheless　　　③ nor　　　④ otherwise　　　〈立命館大〉

# Optional Lesson 6 前置詞

**1** ( )内から正しいほうを選びなさい。 A

1. A straight line is the shortest distance (among / between) 2 points.
2. Why do you wear that ring (in / on) your first finger?
3. He fell (into / out of) the river when he was getting (through / out of) his canoe.
4. The mountain is about 2,500 meters (above / over) sea level.
5. What are you wearing (below / under) your sweater?
6. Let's swim (across / over) the river.
7. The picture (on / to) the wall looks very nice.

**2** ( )内に at, for, in, on から適語を選んで補いなさい。 B

1. David worked hard and painted the whole house ( ) a day.
2. The movie begins ( ) ten minutes. We'll have to hurry.
3. The coach made the team practice ( ) three hours every day.
4. The meeting starts ( ) 2:30 this afternoon.
5. Some trees lose their leaves ( ) the fall.
6. Many shops are closed ( ) Sundays.

**3** ( )内に下の[ ]内から適切なものを選んで補いなさい。 C

1. The boy tried to be a man, but tears came to his eyes ( ) the pain.
2. My grandmother has modern ideas, ( ) her great age.
3. In most schools children are taught ( ) age groups.
4. You should talk to your teacher ( ) just complaining to me about it.
5. We escaped ( ) a secret tunnel.
   [according to, because of, by means of, in spite of, instead of]

**4** ( )内の語句を並べかえ, 英文を完成しなさい。 総合

1. If you hadn't been in such a hurry, you wouldn't have put (instead / into / of / sugar / the sauce) salt.

2. Did you come to London (for / of / seeing / the purpose / your family), or for business purposes?

**Try** ( )内を補うのに最も適切なものを①〜④の中から選びなさい。

1. According ( ) a recent survey, Kobe is one of the best places to live. 〈関西学院大〉
   ① in ② on ③ to ④ with
2. My client and I sat ( ) the table from each other. 〈日本大〉
   ① across ② at ③ in front of ④ to

# Optional Lesson **7** 否定

**1** 次の英文を和訳しなさい。　　　　　　　　　　　　　　　　　　　　Ａ Ｂ

1. Not all children like apples.

2. I am not always free on Sundays.

3. Would you like to come with us? —— I'm afraid not.

4. My mother never goes shopping at the department store without buying a lot.

**2** 次の意味になるように，（　　）内に適語を補いなさい。　　　　　　　　Ｃ

1. まもなくウェブ上で注文した本が届くだろう。
   It won't be (　　　　　　) before the books I ordered on the Web arrive.
2. 人は，健康を失って初めてそのありがたみがわかる。
   We do not know the value of health (　　　　　) we lose it.
3. 彼はけっしてお金を盗むような人ではない。
   He is the (　　　　　) man to steal the money.
4. 物理学は私には理解できない。
   Physics is (　　　　　) my understanding.
5. 彼女の講義は決して退屈ではなかった。
   Her lecture was (　　　　　) but boring.

**3** （　　）内から正しいほうを選びなさい。　　　　　　　　　　　　　総合

1. The performance was far (of / from) being perfect.
2. *A:* I wouldn't say I don't watch TV, but I prefer listening to music.
   *B:* Me too.　I hardly (ever / often) watch TV these days.
3. They were really shocked at the news.　They could (hardly / seldom) speak.

**Try** （　　）内の語句を並べかえ，英文を完成しなさい。

1. I (cannot / running into / someone / this street / walk along / without) I know.
   〈近畿大〉

2. Her (that / presence / so / I / hardly / could / me / overwhelmed) talk.　〈龍谷大〉

# Optional Lesson 8 さまざまな構文

**1** （　）内の指示に従って書きかえなさい。　　　　　　　　　　　　　A

1. Last year I visited Canada, and Mary visited Canada, too.　（下線部にsoを用いて）

2. (a)Jane paid for (b)the meal (c)yesterday.　（下線部(a)〜(c)のそれぞれを強調した文に）
   (a)
   (b)
   (c)

3. Paul didn't get any sleep and his mother didn't either.　（下線部にneitherを用いて）

4. Ordinary people make history.　（下線部を強調した文に）

**2** （　）内に下の[　]内から適切なものを選んで補いなさい。　　　　　B

1. He gets angry when he loses a game.　He's a poor （　　　　　）.
2. Suddenly, someone gave him a （　　　　　） from behind.
3. The doctor will be here soon to have a （　　　　　） at your ankle.
4. He has decided to study law.　I hope he has made the right （　　　　　）.
   [choice,　look,　loser,　push]

**3** 次の各組の文がほぼ同じ意味になるように，（　）内に適語を補いなさい。　C

1. {
   The family became rich because oil was discovered on their land.
   The （　　　　　） of oil on their land made the family rich.
   }

2. {
   Thanks to the money I inherited, I was able to go on a world cruise.
   The money I inherited （　　　　　） me to go on a world cruise.
   }

3. {
   Because of a leg injury, she couldn't play in the game.
   A leg injury （　　　　　） her from playing in the game.
   }

4. {
   She was too proud to accept help.
   Her （　　　　　） didn't allow her to accept help.
   }

5. {
   Because of your words, I felt better.
   Your words （　　　　　） me feel better.
   }

**Try** （　）内を補うのに最も適切なものを①〜④の中から選びなさい。

1. My sister likes playing basketball and so （　　　　　） my brother.　〈会津大〉
   ① is　　　　　② does　　　　　③ has　　　　　④ do

2. Little （　　　　） that I would encounter the Hollywood actor on this backstreet of Tokyo.　〈東海大〉
   ① I have thought　② didn't I think　　③ I haven't thought　④ did I think

# 品詞と文法用語のまとめ

## ≫ 品詞

英文を構成する単語は，それぞれの働きによって主に次の7つの品詞に分類されます。

| 名 | 名 詞 | 人や事物の名前を表す。<br>**Naoko** comes to **school** by **bike**.　（ナオコは自転車で通学します。） |
|---|---|---|
| 代 | 代名詞 | 名詞の代わりに用いられる。I, we, you, he, she, it, theyなど。<br>**She** knows **him**.　（彼女は彼を知っています。） |
| 動 | 動 詞 | 主語の後に続いて，「～します」や「～です」を表す。<br>I **play** tennis every day.　（私は毎日テニスをします。） |
| 形 | 形容詞 | 名詞を修飾したり，主語を説明したりする。<br>She is **happy**.　（彼女は幸せです。） |
| 副 | 副 詞 | 主として動詞を修飾する。<br>Listen to me **carefully**.　（注意して聞きなさい。） |
| 前 | 前置詞 | 名詞や代名詞の前に置かれて，ひとまとまりの意味を表す。<br>at, by, for, in, from, of, on, to, withなど。 |
| 接 | 接続詞 | 語と語，句と句，文と文を結びつける。<br>and, but, or, that, because, when, while, ifなど。 |

## ≫ 文法用語

| be-動詞 | 「…です」にあたるam, are, is, was, were。 |
|---|---|
| 一般動詞 | be-動詞以外のすべての動詞。 |
| 自動詞 | 動作の対象（目的語）を必要としない動詞。 |
| 他動詞 | 動作の対象（目的語）を必要とする動詞。 |
| 現在分詞 | 動詞の～ing形。進行形を作ったり，名詞を修飾したりする。 |
| 過去分詞 | 動詞の-ed形（不規則変化あり）。受動態や完了形を作ったり，名詞を修飾したりする。 |
| 知覚動詞 | 「見る」「聞く」など感覚を表す動詞。see, watch, hear, listen to, feel, noticeなど。 |
| 使役動詞 | 「～させる」という意味の動詞。make, let, have, getなど。 |
| 形式主語 | to-不定詞やthat-節などの代わりに，本来の主語の位置に置かれるitのこと。<br>**It** is dangerous to believe everything on the Internet.<br>（インターネット上のすべてのことを信じるのは危険です。） |
| 形式目的語 | to-不定詞やthat-節などの代わりに，本来の目的語の位置に置かれるitのこと。<br>I found **it** easy to ride a horse.　（私は馬に乗るのは簡単だとわかった。） |